Acclaim for
A GATHERING OF MEN...

Be a Barn Man, that's what I would say to Everyman—father, son, brother, husband and grandfather in America today. After reading this comprehensive guide for building a men's group, I want to buy a copy for every man in my family. A long awaited, much needed, no-nonsense, how-to guide. Truly a book written by and for men in "man speak" to facilitate better communication among men and the people who love them. A guide for building a safe haven where men can learn to share their joys, tragedies and triumphs. This book is written by men for men and is a must-have for the contemporary man and the world he faces today.

—Myrna Allen Cook, Cape Cod, Massachusetts

I read A GATHERING OF MEN with great interest and much gratitude. I am part of a bishop's support group that meets monthly or so—usually six or seven of us—and my experience is much that is recorded here. This book offers this life-giving experience to all who open its pages.

—The Rt. Rev. Charles E. Bennison, Jr.
Bishop, The Episcopal Diocese of Pennsylvania

A sensitive and forthright exposition of how men can, in conventional community, live more discerning and effective lives. A timely antidote to the notion that men, REAL men are from Mars.

—Gerrit W. Kouwenhoven
Civic leader, nonprofit organizations, Dorset, Vermont

I found A GATHERING OF MEN to be provocative and readable. I think it will be immensely useful to those like me who would like to start a group.

—The Rev. Robert T. Brooks
Grace Church, Providence, Rhode Island

A GATHERING OF MEN is an important commentary on the challenges men face as they reflect on their experiences, struggles and successes realized over a lifetime. All too often, men have faced the trials of a life without the sensitive insight of other men. This encouraging book offers an alternative approach wherein a group of men can come together and share of themselves without fear of ridicule and criticism. An appreciation of the value of one's own life and of continued growth is the message. I recommend this book to all men and their loved ones. This book is a must-read for all men.

—Lynmar Brock, Jr.
President and CEO, Brock and Company, Inc.
Man of the Century, Rotary Club of Philadelphia

This book is so informative and helpful. It would be a great text for seminars, for women and men, or for starting a user's group.

—Austin Stern
School Administrator, retired, Brewster, Massachusetts

Father-starved by the industrial revolution, American men have been further abandoned by the jet age dispersal of their families across the continent. Hence, the need for role models, mentoring and connection, which is especially strong as life changes in the retirement years when friends disappear and family obligations diminish.

This spiritually rich book is a how-to-do-it with pearls of wisdom gleaned from ten years of group experience by men committed to each other's growth and welfare.

The rules, values and standards for group maintenance probably developed as a natural selection process when persons not fitting in drop out or refuse to join in the first place and those who adopt the values became loyal and perseverant. But it is well worth the authors' efforts to make the principles explicit, giving group members the chance to define themselves, differentiate from others, and to consciously synthesize their own personality configuration.

—Mark W. Shulkin, MD
Clinical Assistant Professor of Psychiatry
Drexel University College of Medicine

A GATHERING OF MEN

A GATHERING OF MEN

✦

The story of creating a men's group to
address perennial male issues.

Lewis Hartman Mills,
Derek Cornell Stedman,
Robert Clark Wallis

iUniverse, Inc.
New York Lincoln Shanghai

A GATHERING OF MEN

The story of creating a men's group to address perennial male issues.

iUniverse books may be ordered through booksellers or by contacting:

iUniverse
2021 Pine Lake Road, Suite 100
Lincoln, NE 68512
www.iuniverse.com
1-800-Authors (1-800-288-4677)

ISBN-13: 978-0-595-40865-8 (pbk)
ISBN-13: 978-0-595-85229-1 (ebk)
ISBN-10: 0-595-40865-6 (pbk)
ISBN-10: 0-595-85229-7 (ebk)

Printed in the United States of America

"Become more aware of the things in life that really matter:
those that gladden the heart,
refresh the spirit and lift the consciousness."

Findhorn community in Scotland

In Memory of
Lewis Hartman Mills
(1932–2002)

Dedicated to
George L. Barnes
Harry T. Hare
Morton Howard
Howard Kellogg
Carter L. Leidy, Jr.
William J. Shepherd
James Simmons
Joseph W. Wear
William White

Special Thanks

To our wives, Amory H. Stedman and Margaret B. Wallis,
for affirming the importance of the Barn Men
and our efforts.

Contents

Although we are breaking our own rule, the Barn Men
decided to include actual names and conversations,
in the interest of a more accurate portrayal of the men and their thinking.

Preface

A GATHERING OF MEN is about men committed to searching for wisdom and using their discoveries to be better men. The members are bound by mutual concern, honesty and trust. Through the course of meeting regularly, the participants become more aware of and more connected to the real world in which each man lives. Our goal is to achieve deeper self-understanding and meaningful conversation centered on perennial male issues.

Women tend to open discussions on personal issues much more easily than men. This book is an effort to encourage men to grow in the company of other men. The three authors belong to a men's group that has been meeting twice a month for more than ten years. The reader will hear the voice of each author as the chapters unfold. Each amplifies the group experience yet brings a unique personal quality to the tale when told. As other men read these pages, it is hoped they, too, will discover the group experience as a means of effectively closing gaps in their own lives through the enduring friendships that evolve in a group where open dialogue is encouraged.

A GATHERING OF MEN suggests a format for meetings while understanding that each group of men must establish its own guiding principles. The guidelines included here are more general than specific, both philosophical and practical.

A GATHERING OF MEN is a unique book in that it was written by men who broke new ground. No other men's group could be modeled. None of the charter members or those men later assimilated into the group had participated in a group quite like the Barn Men. This group of men continues to meet because there is no other forum where a man can convene with peers and speak about any topic meaningful to him and know his ideas, his feelings and his inner self will be respected and appreciated with full knowledge that his words will be held in strict confidence by the entire group.

The personal perspectives in *A GATHERING OF MEN* offer ways that individual lives have been enriched by the experience of a shared journey.

Lew Mills (deceased)
Derek Stedman
Bob Wallis

Foreword
Genesis of a Men's Group

Time for reflection is often a luxury for men. The pursuit of goals as the means of success is hammered hard. But life on the fast track can be barren. Life lived in pursuit of future achievement can diminish present pleasure. Men chase expectations like carousel brass rings, when, in fact, the treasures they possess are worth far more. Life's unseen treasures are simple: good health, a pretty day, a special memory, a job well done, an unexpected kindness—given or received, these are gems that remain unnoticed when life's journey is lived as a timed event. Men approaching middle age often reach a point when they long to savor life rather than race it.

Some members of a group known as the Barn Men, i.e., they began meeting in an old barn, offer this account of what drew them together and what their fellowship means to them.

The common thread of the Barn Men is the cultural imperative that reared them to win, to be responsible, to survive, and to follow the social sanctions about their use of time. These sanctions regard slowing down as a waste of time, time dedicated to friendship as unproductive and time taken from action to explore feelings and motivations as "wimpy". Such models of male behavior rob men of the ability to savor precious moments, *carpe diem*, without guilt. Their intention is to broaden self-awareness, strengthen relationships with spouses and children, gain close friends, deepen their spiritual lives, seek wisdom, become better men, and to take the time to do it.

Each man's story is sufficiently similar to serve as convincing evidence that men in a fast paced society share a void. In exploring their mutual dilemma, the Barn Men recognized the insights they have gained could be useful for other men. The plaintive cries of isolation, loneliness and confusion expressed in these obvious quotations are not new but the void they expose is more prevalent today.

"If this is the greatest time to be alive and I have so much, why am I still searching?"

"I'm lonely; everyone around me seems to be connected to family, job and friends."

"I notice women function differently. They have friends with whom they share and examine events in their lives. They remain in close contact and support one another."

"I wonder if other men feel as isolated as I?"

"It's my experience that telling feelings to other men often results in sarcasm or humor intended as a put down. It's been that way since grammar school."

"I think of myself as an eight cylinder car running on one."

"My family had secrets, secrets about depression. I was an adult before I learned of my father's clinical depression which decked him when his father died. All I knew as a child was that he was very remote and, for me, unapproachable."

"I would have enjoyed an old-fashioned apprenticeship. A chance to be guided by a mentor and molded in a way that gave a clear understanding of what was expected of me."

"I'm lonely. I miss the extended family gatherings of my childhood."

"I don't want to hang myself out and whine, but I do want to search for a more intentional way of living. I want to get unstuck and make a difference."

"I miss the camaraderie and open-ended questioning of college."

"My father was always distant. As I entered adolescence and was attempting to know him, he died; I 'handled' it inside, on my own. My feelings of loss were buried deep within me."

"I attended church and the hymns and prayers were uplifting; the sermon often did more to shut me down than open me up. I felt 'talked at'."

"I would like to know my children better."

"I want to know more about how I can protect and nurture life in my place on Earth."

"I want to know God's will in my life."

As society becomes more fragmented socially, professionally, physically and spiritually, clearly articulated community values are drowned out by the stark isolation of modern society. In an age in which anything goes, we have reached a point where we fail to stand for anything.

Well-defined principles of community are clouded by the notion that there is benefit to being separate, apart. Most men come together in competitive environments that lack opportunities to build trusting friendships. Manly friendships that have heretofore served as the glue of civilization, have been replaced in a suspicious, dog-eat-dog climate. The bedrock of individual character has become a pebbled beach of countless options lacking any basis for discernment absent the caring feedback of trusted friends.

As society embraces rugged individualism, the essentials of community are eroding. In an environment where sharing wisdom and reaching out to another in trust is regarded as unmanly, men hurl themselves into wrenching encounters alone. The Barn Men have found a better way.

Eleanor Boggs Shoemaker
Editor

1

Bob: There is Something Missing in My Life

Pinocchio's Restaurant on a blustery February day seemed a good place for Carter and me to lunch. Recently having taken a job twenty miles away from most of my friends, Pinocchio's afforded a brief break in the work routine. Carter and I had each experienced divorce and remarriage. We met several years ago through our new spouses who had been friends since elementary school.

Most of my men friends are task oriented—one is a great remodeler, others love sports and a growing number enjoy cooking. All are wonderful and fun when we are mutually engaged in an activity. But when the activity ceases, meaningful conversations quite often also cease. Carter has another gift—he is a spectacular listener. When he gains an insight or a new idea, or, even better, a question, he doesn't let go of it. He holds on, picks it up, chews on it, lets it rest, picks it up again and then revisits it a month or so later. Our conversations have real depth as we truly explore ideas.

Usually when I have lunch with a buddy and mention it to my wife, she may make a personal inquiry such as, "How is he getting on without his dear, old dog?"

I admit I don't know. I did not even know his dog had died; perhaps, I was not even aware he had a dog. Task-oriented, project-driven friends have interesting conversations, but they seldom include personal experiences. Often men's worlds touch, but only on the surface.

Few of my conversations go very deeply with anyone except my wife. I notice women function differently. They confide in their spouses, but they also count on special women friends with whom they maintain close contact. Their friendships evidence genuine concern for one another. I thought, as a man, I might be unusual in longing for that sort of affirming, male friendships. I didn't have a clue if any of my male friends sought to gain more from friendship than games

1

and sports and a good laugh. My men friends did not share anything other than very superficial aspects of their lives. Neither did I.

I decided I would like to have a friend who would share honest dialogue. I also knew I would not risk exposing my feelings to just anyone. I had experienced what it was like to speak openly and then feel unheard. The listener would change the subject, reply with a sarcastic retort, or make a joke to conceal his discomfort at any acknowledgment of feelings. There is nothing like sarcasm to stem heart-felt expressions. I experienced this in grade school and high school, as have most men.

Worse than the immediate effect of sarcasm is its long-term impact, the shutting down of reactions and feelings in selfdefense. Such defense mechanisms engender avoidance of emotions. As a teenager I read Sloan Wilson's novel, *The Man in the Grey Flannel Suit*. The protagonist is a disillusioned, friendless businessman who harbors a secret and masks the pain of his stagnant, isolated life in obsessive work which unsettles his marriage. I knew I wasn't masking feelings very well when a friend observed that I appeared to him like an eight cylinder car running on one cylinder; a direct assessment and a wake up call. My first reaction was pique, but upon reflection I acknowledged the truth of his observation and considered the source of what was now obvious to others, my anxiety.

I was functional at home and work, but I lacked spontaneity. I felt an angst I could not define. Sometimes my sleep was interrupted by concern for a distant child; or my aging mother whom I loved, but who frustrated me and elicited ambivalent feelings by placing increasing demands on my time. An employee could get under my skin. I was "bottled up". As all of these feelings festered within me, I remained committed to "a stiff upper lip" and "to keep marching." I thought this was the way a man was to live and compete successfully, but it was taking a toll. As this awareness took hold, I began a search that resulted in the formation of the Barn Men.

There had to be a better way. My wife could not be responsible for my psycho-social needs. We have mutual interests and share a deep love, but unloading pent-up emotions on her would not enliven our marriage. The volcano I was fighting to contain could overwhelm our relationship. A wife cannot provide another male's views on a topic. Nor is a wife particularly interested in everything her husband is thrashing around with in his gut. A topic may not even be comprehensible by the opposite sex.

A serendipitous walk among the stacks at a bookstore provided the inspiration I was seeking. *Iron John: A Book About Men*, by Robert Bly, caught my eye. I later learned he is credited as the father of what is known as the "expressive men's movement." Bly advocates men's groups which encourage dialogue.

Each page of his book validated the isolation men face in modern society. I had heard of a church-sponsored gathering of men, but each time I raised the possibility of starting such a group with my pastor, it went nowhere. Later, I raised the subject with the rector of another church. He jumped on the idea and formed a men's group. Unfortunately, the rector's purpose and mine were not in sync. He viewed the men's group as a means to gain support for parish projects—no surprise, I suppose.

I spent a lot of time commuting in my car listening to the radio. Music relaxes me. There is nothing quite like hearing *Red, Red Wine* on the steel drums and mentally escaping to a dance floor where everyone is moving to the same rhythm. Listening to music in the car provided temporary relief for my feelings of isolation and confusion but no new perspectives. Trying to breach the sense of isolation was like cutting grass, going back and forth over the same ground.

I tried meditation and yoga with good results. The mindfulness elicits a sense of quiet and a broader vision of reality. Taking a deep breath—a two-minute stretch—removed the tension of the moment. I was able to resume the task at hand refreshed and less weary, but still no wiser.

I think I would have enjoyed an apprenticeship with an old master cabinetmaker, a skillful horse trainer or a canny lawyer who mentored the next generation. They were guides who were masters of their crafts willing to coach and encourage a young man. Neophytes learned subtle skills and useful business practices from those caring leaders who praised and scolded as required. A teacher who is wise and caring makes learning a wonderful experience.

My extended family is scattered far and wide. One brother lives in another state and one lives abroad. Both of my parents are dead. Aunts, uncles and cousins are scattered all over the place. I miss the opportunity of informal visits, but we do gather on holidays and have lots of fun. The get-togethers reinforce a sense of family identity and rekindle traditions of parents and grandparents. They connect me with my roots. As a child it was Sunday dinner at my grandparents' house where I came to know my mother's family and the personalities in it. The most fun was being with cousins as we raked leaves or played tag. I gained a sense of family and learned family lore which contributed to the man I am today.

As Carter and I spoke over lunch that cold February day at Pinocchio's, I shared my frustration. I asked, "Why is it our wives get together and share concerns with their women friends, but men avoid substantive conversations?" Carter said the question resonated with similar thoughts of his. He expressed a wish to explore the way other men wanted to be remembered, or if given a month off, where they would go and what they would like to do; or he would like to know about other men's fathers. I agreed. I wanted to be in a group like the ones I experienced in college where we debated history, analyzed personality types, solved lab questions and sometimes just *hung out*. Those college gatherings covered lots of ground and there were no bounds. Lifestyles were questioned. Values were examined and defined. It had been an inspiring time. There was a lot of dialogue. I missed the stimulating, thought-provoking conversations. Such times had now become far too infrequent in my life.

Carter agreed. That day we decided to assemble a group of men who also were keenly interested in coming to grips with a wide range of genuine topics. Both Carter and I began by contacting friends and they in turn had friends who all possessed abiding interests in sincerely exploring wide ranges of authentic issues in men's lives. The individuals drew together from that day to create the group shortly to be known as the Barn Men.

Reflections:

- Have you a void in your life?

- Can you describe it?

- Have you a male friend who is experiencing a void in his life?

- Have you discussed it?

- Have you a mentor?

- Have you a male friend with whom you have discussed fathers?

- Would you like more dialogue in your life?

- Would you like to have a spiritual dimension in your life?

2

Derek: What is missing?

A gastroenterologist put his finger on my continuing ulcer pains: "It isn't what you are eating; it is all about what's eating you." I didn't know how to tell him what was, and more importantly, what was not going on in my life. He was absolutely correct in his diagnosis, but how could I name what was eating away at me? What was missing in my life creating the ragged emptiness festering in my gut? My upbringing regarded self reliance as manly. How could I look outside of myself? This bizarre male problem-solving paradigm of seeking to fill interior voids on my own was clearly ridiculous. What could I use for filling the inside when I had nothing on the inside or the outside?

Everyone around me seemed so well connected to family, job and friends and seemed to be going along just fine. Why was I the "odd man out?" Being odd man out is a very lonely feeling.

I recalled an anecdote my wife's cousin had shared. The story goes that a burgee emblazoned with the appellation, "Figawe", flies aloft the marquee of a popular bistro on the south shore of Cape Cod. Local aficionados delight in explaining its meaning. *Figawe* was first heard over a ship to shore radio. It was uttered by the distraught skipper of a newly acquired power boat somewhere in Buzzard's Bay. He had invited friends aboard for a fishing trip. The day was hot and humid with poor visibility and the fish weren't biting. After a few hours all on board agreed they were ready to go ashore. But the proud skipper was in trouble. He had traveled beyond sight of land and the unread navigation manuals, still wrapped in cellophane, reposed in the boot of his car on shore. A shipmate produced AAA road maps which noted ferryboat routes to Martha's Vineyard and Nantucket. They were of little help. The skipper veered one way then another assuring his passengers they would catch sight of land and reach port shortly. His friends, all erstwhile "landlubbers," considered mutiny but didn't know what it would achieve since none was any better equipped to guide the boat ashore. As each man grasped the gravity of the situation, reason sank, panic rose and the hapless skipper continued looking unsuccessfully for sight of land. At last the captain, bereft of self confidence, acknowledged his predicament, engaged the ship to shore radio and began frantically shouting "Figawe?" "Figawe?" As the cry traveled across the airwaves, other sailors responded and guided the ship safely to shore. When the rescued men were at anchor, they headed for the bistro and toasted their heroes. Now when visitors inquire, "What does that 'Figawe' banner mean?" the locals delight in recounting the story which in Massachusetts parlance means, "Where the frig are we?"

"Figawe?" rang true for me. Where was I? How could I find solid ground? Like the men at sea, I was compelled to ask for guidance. My inadequacy had, at last, dawned on me. My notion of self-sufficiency: find a solution for me, by myself, without anyone else's advice or input was absurd. I know many men who also approach problems this way. What is it that leads us to reach out beyond ourselves for new solutions is the same factor that forces the lost skipper to cry out for help? Desperation.

Desperation initially keeps men attempting to reach a successful resolution by repeating over and over the same thing which did not work in the first place. Keep driving our "boats" around in circles until divine intervention steps in to rescue us? Nope. Life does not seem to work that way. Eventually we learn that course of action does not work.

The Barn Men offers a benign forum to a man before he approaches feeling desperate. The Barn Men meeting format provides multiple opportunities for every member to share minor to major internal and external shake-ups to his operating systems. Each man has brought a significant problem and/or question to the group.

We have shared a man's dreadful uneasiness about who may sleep with his wife after he dies. Increasing incidents of apparent impotence have been nervously brought up and then to the speaker's great relief, the other men acknowledge similar feelings and events associated with drooping "performance" levels. Panic from anticipated cancer pain, pre and post brain surgery worries, opinions on homosexuality, "fast-forwarding" to a spouse's declining health, the death of one's youthful daughter.

The horrors which ensnare our wee hours of the morning when we "should" be sleeping provide opportunities for communal recognition and open conversation. Try sharing your innermost thoughts about these real-time shocks to one's system and most men I know other than the Barn Men will either turn away from that unexpected intrusion on their walled-in defensive listening, turn the conversation to anything else or look dumbfounded and extricate themselves as fast as possible to another place where "safer" talk can once again insulate them from the actualities of life.

There is huge, mutual trust among the Barn Men which has been given and earned and shared over our many hours together. Over time we have learned how to listen, how to ease out the circumstances surrounding a man's feelings and thoughts and how not to give "answers' but to help the speaker explore his own, newly-found solutions.

Sometimes the notion of trusting someone other than yourself surfaces in a memory. My grandfather made me his project as I struggled through teenage years. He taught me to fly fish and twice took me away to his fishing camp in the northern Canadian woods. He provided environs away from New York City, the place I lived and despised. He made me welcome at his farm. He showed me how to perform farm chores. He worked beside me and encouraged me as we did hard, dirty work. He taught me to play golf, swim in the wild ocean surf, play cards with his pals and to be comfortable with adults. I admired him and respected him. I worked hard for him. I learned so much from him. I adored him. I trusted him and, I deeply regret, never told him.

I didn't know how to express my feelings. My boyish reflection illustrates the palliative effect of being the focus of someone's undivided attention. The gracious concern of another is always a factor in enhanced self evaluation. Being cared for and having someone give us jump starts when we need them helps us reach a point where we want to pass that kind of care forward to others.

I miss the intimacy of my grandfather's friendship. I feel disconnected from that kind of closeness with my family and friends. Intimacy is a rare experience for me. Whom do I really know? Scary thoughts for which I had no answers. I wonder if most young children have such sweet intimacies only to lose them in the process of reaching adulthood? I want to reconnect with others and the world around me. I want to integrate myself in the human plan. But what is the plan?

Benjamin Franklin also sought male kinship in eighteenth century Philadelphia. He organized a group he called the Junto. It had no esoteric purpose. The men gathered to examine assumptions and provide one another with feedback. Of the group Franklin wrote,"I find I love company, chat, a laugh, a glass and even a song." One biographer, Edmund S. Morgan observes "Franklin's consuming curiosity about the world and what made it tick extended to the people in it, accompanied by a delight in being one of them. As he enjoyed watching the ways of the world, he enjoyed simply being with its people, sharing thoughts with them, feeling affection for them, laughing with them, and finding out who they were and who he himself was." And why not? This is, in fact, what I seek: to know others better and myself as well.

Historian Arnold Toynbee observed that of the twenty-one great civilizations on earth, the modern West is the first that does not have or teach its citizens any answer to the question of why they exist. This Western societal failure begins in the home. Maurice Sendak observed "Parents no longer tell children things. They do not tell the clear facts that we have to learn as we grow up. We have to find out things because they don't tell us." Bewildered parents struggling with their own isolation fail to establish guidelines and children are left to figure life out alone.

The supreme good of life, the *summum bonum*, is not easily experienced or observed; it is learned through sharing. The loving transfer of what is good and true passes from one generation to the next more easily than the painful trial and error of individual experimentation which modern society mandates. Values only defined and implemented by peers, absent the influence of previous generations, leave much to be desired by way of conventional wisdom.

Maslow's work offers an assessment of fully functional adults, those whom he identifies as self actualizing. He describes such individuals as being equipped with healthy world views which result in actions based on positive motivations yielding satisfaction. A laudable goal, but when the external support to facilitate that level of maturity is lacking, the achievement of Maslow's maturity pinnacle is not possible. Self actualization without external models and initial support is impossible. Without empowering models of caring attentive adults, young people atrophy in perpetual states of adolescent narcissism. Men deprived of positive, mature, male role models can seek clarification and validation in caring male fellowships but the process begins, ironically, with oneself.

Friendship, an essential ingredient in self actualized lives, is elusive. Friendships constitute a means of establishing cooperative communities. History holds fascinating accounts of the merits of friendship as well as the disastrous results of friendship gone awry. C.S. Lewis explores the components of friendship in his work, *The Four Loves*. He asserts "Friendship arises from common insights, interests, tastes, truths. Friends share visions and care about the same truths. Friendship is a shoulder to shoulder journey that is shared. Friendships are about something." He maintains those not part of the relationship can feel excluded.

Lewis concludes that people can exist without friendship, but they live with a sense of isolation when they do. Though durable friendship is not a panacea for the challenges of life, it is certainly an undeniable strengthening element for coping with life's obstacles. Establishing an enduring friendship, philos, is less problematic than establishing an enduring relationship predicated on romantic attachment, eros. Since friendship is an outgrowth of common interest and shared values, there is less stress than in relationships based on romantic involvement the source of which partly is physical attraction. Friendship is more rational, but in today's society it is also, curiously, more rare.

I learned more of what I know about friendship from fellow author, Lew Mills. As we became very close friends through Barn Men meetings and subsequent collaboration on this book, I observed and participated in the dynamics of friendship formation.

Lew was a take-little-for-granted kind of guy. He challenged statements of fellow Barn Men. He scoffed at platitudes and demanded thoughtful exchanges. He required us to think. Lew communicated very well and from deep within himself. He sometimes irked people with his searching dialog. However, as I grew to know Lew better and better, I appreciated and respected his ways of thinking and speaking more and more. He eschewed superficial communication and avoided mindless chit chat. He wanted to really know others, particularly those whom he regarded as true friends.

If I recounted a tale of a hairy sail, he wanted me to go beyond telling the wind speed, heel of the vessel or what sails were used. He encouraged me to share my interior experience of the event…what I felt during the adventure. He wanted a penetrating glimpse into my reality.

He was open and he expected others to be open as well. His heart was big and he wore it on his sleeve. He was vulnerable. Being vulnerable to others was an integral step on Lew's path of creating true friendships for himself. He thoroughly enjoyed being himself. He encouraged everyone to drop the façade of hail fellow well met.

I trusted Lew enough to let him know me, warts and all. He was such a trusting person. He was so exposed and we were all drawn to his openness. I discovered another missing part of myself, openness. I was fearful that openness might bring rejection, but learned through Lew that openness in friendship brings concern and affirmation through sharing the real "stuff" of life with friends.

As my friendship with Lew deepened, he faced the final challenge of his life. Lew was dying painfully of cancer. Through his church friends, his neighbors, the Barn Men and others we hauled Lew up and down stairs. We took him on turbulent rides in his wheelchair over the snow-covered front lawn to get him to his radiation treatments. Tears and laughter mixed frequently as we jiggled and juggled him around. On good days Lew would demand loudly, "Get me a good cup of real coffee. Real stand-up stuff I can smell and taste!"

We held Barn Men meetings at his house when he became too debilitated to leave home. Tears flowed freely as together we endured his departure from our lives. But as usual, Lew strengthened our lives during this time by sharing his evolving feelings and ideas. "What I realize is happening to me," revealed Lew, "is that while my physical body is growing slighter and slighter, my spiritual body is growing and growing! I am just trading one for the other. The best is yet to come!"

To a man we felt the terrible pain of loss when Lew died. But we celebrated the gift of having known him as a true friend.

Life is never static. As I continue to move through my life, I recognize the importance of examining where I am along the way. The question, "What is missing in my life?", is less daunting now. Because of Lew I have dared to look into the voids and face them. I have discovered the comfort of knowing I am not alone. A friend is a mirror that encourages me to search. When I do, I see a reflection of what I had for so long thought was my singular experience; in friendship I recognize the commonality of life experience. I am not alone.

Reflections:

• Can you identify "holes" in your life?

• Whom do you trust?

• Whom do you mentor?

3

Lew: How Do I Begin? Getting Started with Myself

Most men I know want more out of life than they are getting. The "more" is different for each of us. It often includes a spiritual dimension of the human journey; that is, those moments filled with awe, mystery and wonder for which there are no words of explanation. Then there is the occasional flash, a brief nanosecond when we understand all that we see, taste, touch, smell and hear, but that does not account for what is happening to us. Sometimes we are intensely aware that our reality is not all there is. Such yearnings are muted in youth but intensify by midlife and, for many, become a high priority in the later years. Even so, I believe many men fail to move from the desire for "more" to acting on their desire. I have been curious about this not only as a witness of other men but in trying to understand my own resistance to what I believe would enrich and enhance my life. I am convinced that if I could "get going" on this journey, my relationships, especially with those whom I love, would be more direct, infused with honesty and just plain better.

So what is it that keeps men (including the author) from "getting going?" Why is it so hard to get started? What I am going to say is not new, or especially profound, but it contains truth for me. The reader may find some of my observations will mirror some of theirs.

Inertia

A long time ago, I bought a little round toy that had a tag, which said, "This is a Round Tuit." Inertia is the force that says, "I'll get around to it" one of these days. But, of course, that day seldom, if ever, comes. Inertia is a silent wall, a barrier that stunts lives and saps creative energy. The problem with inertia is that what might have happened and what does happen are eons apart. Much of what a man could do, what I could have done, is left undone because of simple inertia.

In my religious tradition there is a prayer which grieves over the "things done that I should not have done, and the things left undone that I should have done." It is the things left undone that are the products of inertia.

Habit

My morning routine is just about the same day after day, week after week, year after year. I pull out the shaving cream, apply it to my face in exactly the same sequence and then move the razor this way and that in very defined and repeated patterns. Then comes the toothbrush, worked on this tooth and the rest in an order which never puts one molar ahead of another. Next come the pills, the hairbrush and finally the T-shirt, left until all the splashing is done. There are dozens of places in my life where habit takes over, most of the time without my being conscious of it at all. Habit locks out all sorts of other possibilities. Habit is often a mini-prison and a serious block to innovation in life. I have often heard coworkers explain, "We have always done it this way." Habit is the antithesis of innovation. It is condensed resistance to being open to the unexpected and serendipitous in life. It dulls the blade, dampens the fire and dilutes the vigor of life. "Habitual living" is an oxymoron.

Time

"How can I get started on the 'more' if I haven't the time?" I have a fine Steinway grand piano in the living room. I thoroughly enjoy practicing, taking lessons and gaining competence at the keyboard. In the last couple of months, my fingers have seldom hit the ivories. Why? It isn't that I don't have time. It's because I don't take time. Other things come first. Gardening, writing my memoirs, riding my bike, lunching with friends, sleeping in–all these get done. But the piano just sits there. My excuse is often that I don't have time. But, it is an excuse.

Sure, my life is crammed full of things that I want to do, and I make time to do them. It isn't easy to reorder my priorities to make time for music. I know pleading the cause of no time robs me of the delight of making music and gaining skill. The same plea can and often does divert my attention from searching for the "more" in life.

I'm Too Old Now

"You can't teach an old dog new tricks," is an old saw that prevents a lot of men from starting in a new direction. "Well, a lot of water has gone over the dam, I'm a senior citizen, a golden-ager—" all such statements dismiss the possibility of new life using the excuse of having lived sixty or seventy years. The older I get the more I realize that chronology is one of the least accurate measurements of age. Spirit, attitude, a sense of adventure, a willingness to see each day as a gift, all of those rate higher in my understanding of what it means to be alive and to be older. I have met twenty-year-old men who seem old and eighty-year-old men who are full of life and expectation. If you think you are too old to get started on a new way of living, think again. Remember, it isn't how long you live, but how you live that is important.

If I Change, Does That Mean I've Been Wrong All These Years?

Not long ago I had a knee operated on by a method called arthoscopy. This is a non-invasive, highly successful procedure that is done on an out-patient basis. Only a few years ago the same doctor would have to have made large incisions in my knee in a much longer procedure that would have required hospitalization and a lengthy recovery. Did the new procedure mean the old method was wrong?

When I began visiting a lovely island in Maine, we used Coleman lanterns, hauled water from the lake and had no way of communicating with the mainland. Now cell phones, solar power panels and a gas pump at the lake make life far easier. The old ways were hard, but they were not wrong. The new ways give us more time to enjoy the surf or to sit and read. It's the same in our lives as men. Altering ways of the past that we cling to with affection does not need to imply anything was wrong with the past. It is simply a recognition that we may have found a better way of doing something. Make friends with change.

I Might Fail

Yes, you might fail. Someone told me one time, "The only risk you can't afford to take is no risk at all." Fear of failure stymies many men, diverts their energy and boxes them into shallow, narrow existences. Worry about being humiliated, losing face or appearing less masculine often stops men from taking steps to grow.

I have a good friend whose father chipped away at his self-confidence for as long as he could remember. He could never do anything right in his father's eyes and his father never failed to point out his flaws. Now in his middle fifties, he is stuck, unable to make critical decisions about his life, his relationships and his own future. His father is dead, but my friend is still immobilized by the fear of disapproval and failure his father instilled in him. Such fear can turn to terror and stall a deeper, richer life.

Fear of Vulnerability

What if I find things out about myself that I don't like? What happens if other people know things about me that I have always kept secret? Will I lose control over myself? How will I deal with finding out that others may discover I am not as good as I have led them to believe?

Joining a men's group and being honest with oneself and others can be frightening. In most cultures, if a man seems vulnerable, he is viewed as weak, inadequate, even feminine. Most men work hard to "keep up a front" and that is what it is. Perhaps the only one being fooled is oneself. I believe deep in the hearts of men there is a desire to be real, authentic, honest and open. I believe, given the chance and enough support, most men would choose to live deeper, more meaningful, lives infused with energy.

A Few Thoughts On Getting Started

Remember, what you know about yourself is not all there is. Did you ever say to yourself, "Why did I say or do that?" "Where did that thought originate?" "Why am I feeling this way?"

Much of our life is spent in the conscious, every day world. But there is a lot more to each of us than we can see, taste, touch, hear or smell. I believe most men would like a better idea of who we are, and that desire can be sufficient motivation to move us on to learning more and becoming more whole. Taking time to be curious about how we got to be who we are can be the beginning of a richer life.

Pay attention to dreams, hunches and even memories that pop in mind. Dreams are compensatory messages that point to something in our conscious lives. Everybody dreams now and then, and dreams are gold mines of information. Dreams are most often couched in a code language and require work to make sense of them. Ferreting out the message of a dream is gathering information that can lead to a better understanding of ourselves. Ask big questions: "Who am I? How did I get here? What am I here for, and what is next for me?" There are no right or wrong answers but questions can get you off dead center and onto new discoveries.

Acknowledge that life on this planet is a gift you have been given. Making the most of who and what you are is an expression of, "thank you". Think of life as a gift and seek ways to be a thanks-giving person. This idea will bring new insights and energize your entire being.

Most of us could benefit from a healthy sense of urgency. Our life on Earth is brief. With that in mind, we will, at every age, not put off doing things we deem important for ourselves or others.

A major task of every life is to grow up. I am convinced it is a life-long work. When we reach a point where we consciously decide the time has come to really grow up, we begin to live very differently.

These thoughts may break personal logjams and move us into action. There is always more we can do. To find what we are to do does, however, require that we get started.

It's A Work In Progress

"Getting started" is a work in progress. It is a lifetime task. The alternative is stagnation and a premature, psychic death. Life is a journey—an adventure, an exploration, a quest. And it's there, waiting for us.

Lew: Thoughts for Men to Ponder

- Who was your father?

- Did you know him?

- Did he know you?

- Who needs me?

- If I die tomorrow, will anyone miss me? Who?

- How do I want to be remembered?

- How will I be remembered?

- If I could change one thing about myself, what would it be?

- What emotion/behavior do I express most frequently?

- What emotion/behavior would I like to express more effectively?

4

Bob: Gathering the Group

In *Dry Salvages*, T. S. Eliot highlights the difficulty of exposing personal truths when he writes, "These are only hints and guesses, hints followed by guesses; and the rest is prayer, observance, discipline, thought and action." If, I don't risk uncovering "hints and guesses," "right action" cannot occur. And Eliot maintains that action yields the freedom to live.

Several of us began exploring ways we might gather a group of interested men and how we could organize regular meetings. We were fortunate in knowing several people who were willing to meet with us and share their groups' work formats and experiences. As a result we put together some helpful meeting guidelines (see later in this chapter) which have served us well.

Carter and I began checking the interest levels of other men. Joe, a cancer survivor, had facilitated new member groups in a Wellness Community. One of his friends, Cindy, belonged to a co-ed gathering. Cindy offered to meet with several of us over lunch near her office. Joe's brother-in-law had attended personal growth seminars over the years and was enthusiastic about our group. We wanted to approach another friend, but we doubted if he would be interested. He proved us wrong and even offered a cozy room with a wood-burning fireplace in his small barn as a meeting place.

It was perfect. It also gave us our informal name, the Barn Men. The five of us accepted Cindy's invitation to talk over lunch about forming a group. Another man, Peter, a Quaker, offered to meet with us one evening. During the meeting Peter noticed our discomfort when silence descended on the group and suggested we try a five-minute silence to overcome our awkwardness about it. We did, and the use of silence was launched.

We began meeting in Jody's barn with the doors thrown open to capture bird songs on a June evening in 1995, four months after the luncheon at Pinocchio's. One original member was with us for six months, but business travel interrupted his attendance too often for him to feel enough continuity with Barn Men conversations. Another man was with us for several years but his narrow perspective was in tension with the Barn Men's commitment to an unbounded spiritual search.

Others joined the Barn Men along the way. One day at a local dry cleaning store, I ran into an old friend and former boss whose wife had always urged him to try meeting with a group. He accepted our invitation and until recently was our eldest member.

Sometimes discussion of Barn Men meetings surface during dinner conversations with friends. The significance of the Barn Men in our lives is hard not to mention. Occasionally this leads to a man expressing interest in joining. Two members, one an old friend of a Barn Man, new to the area, joined simultaneously. A third man, a wonderful introspective, philosophical artist, joined a few months later.

More recently a former Episcopal priest and a good friend of a Barn Man, now retired from a City position, welcomed the chance to join.

In the evolution of our fellowship we have found some ingredients that allow our group to work well.

Guidelines, Barn Men Meetings

- Where there is a high level of commitment to the regular meeting.

- Where confidentiality is assumed.

- Where no advice of any kind is offered.

- Where "I" messages are employed rather than "we" or "you" or "one".

- Where no one dominates the conversation, but all risk speaking.

- Where trust, honest conversation and the sharing of feelings have priority.

- Where each openly reflects on the observations of others in truth and love.

- Where differences are discussed in the gathering; never in sub-groups outside the presence of all members.

It is helpful for each member of the fellowship to have a copy of the guidelines at meetings as reminders of group expectations. When we have a guest visitor or a new member joins, we begin the meeting with a review of our guidelines and the assurance that confidences are protected.

Juliet B. Schor, author of *The Overworked American*, notes that lives today are overloaded with so many obligations that conflicts are common. A successful gathering of men must be a priority for each member. Family vacations, very special occasions, or illness are the only valid reasons not to attend. When attendance becomes infrequent, the momentum of relationship-building is lost.

When an individual decides to begin a group, nothing succeeds like trying. Talk up the idea with various men. Identify two or three men in your circle whom you feel are most likely to have an interest in personal growth. Bring it up when you have a little time one-on-one, not at a party. See if the idea sparks any interest. Mention your reasons for wanting to consider this experience. Tell the potential member you will check back with him in a few days. Follow up and find out if he is interested in attending a meeting.

Develop a list of candidates. If your first prospect responds positively to the idea, ask him to make a list and then compare lists. Initially, finding five or six interested men can begin a group with the ultimate goal of ten to twelve members. More than a dozen members can lead to discomfort disguised as humor and one-liner quips—a telltale sign of "dis-ease."

A sense of safety is required for men to open up and be trusting of one another. One hundred percent attendance is unrealistic, so the size of the membership is important.

Characteristics of men who may be interested in joining include:

- Inquisitive

- Reflective

- Open-minded

- Sincere interest in speaking out about topics

All types of men have come to our gathering, introverts and extroverts alike, but all have an interest in searching for truth and a willingness to share. It is hard to guess who will be interested, so you need to talk about the purpose of the group. Some will be clear it is not for them; others will be tentative, but willing to attend a meeting and see. Men approaching fifty or older will probably be the most interested, but don't preclude a thirty-five-year-old, for instance, if he is motivated. Currently the Barn Men range in age from mid-fifties to early seventies.

Diversity contributes to the strength of a group, but too many perspectives and backgrounds can be frustrating. Common past experiences tend to enhance camaraderie. Most of the Barn Men live in different communities in about a twenty mile radius of Philadelphia. That one time when we invited three new members at roughly the same time, there was concern, at first, that three might be too many new faces for a small group; but all three are still with us and have added a lot to our fellowship.

When five or six men have expressed an interest in meeting it's time to begin.

Reminders

- *What is the minimum number to start a group?*

  Five, but eight or nine is preferable—and eventually a dozen is best. When a group exceeds twelve, the level of the trust is diminished. A minimum of three can meet, but five or six is better.

- *What makes a gathering of men grow?*

  A sense of trust established among members who listen and share.

- *Can you ask someone to leave?*

  Rarely, because those who don't value the fellowship will probably drop out of the group. If they do not, however, any decision about membership must be made at a meeting–not by a clique of several members, and never outside the meeting.

- *After the group is established, how are new members selected and invited?*

  Discuss prospective members together. Provide an opportunity for members to share concern before invitations are extended. Ask the group if you may invite the prospective member as a guest. If and when unanimous agreement is reached, proceed with an invitation to attend one meeting without the inference of a long-term membership.

5

Derek: Backgrounds and Foregrounds

As I gain understanding of those who came before me, my own world view is enriched. Reflecting on my background pinpoints my position; where I am, how I got here and where I'm going. As I sort out my life, I am able to determine the "stuff" I want to keep, decide what is missing and put the rest in a discard pile. In seeking perspective as an adult on parents, siblings and previous generations, my view gains objectivity.

Such reflections may elicit a new way of thinking of my parents. Rather than griping about what they did not do for me or complaining about what seemed, at the time, to be injustices, I discover a new view. I can stop complaining and forgive their faults and failures as well as my own. I can move on. Such reflections can be addressed in a fellowship of men. Exploration into the past involves letting go of childish impressions. It involves drawing on spiritual foundations to stop criticizing and complaining and inject unselfish love, an energizing force.

The achievement of acceptance and forgiveness will put me where I want to be energized, alert, open to my surroundings living a here-and-now, real, fulfilling life on Earth. I want to be alert to the signposts along the way.

Signposts

Signpost: "A post bearing a sign that gives information or guidance, any immediately perceptible indication, an obvious clue, etc. To provide a place, route, etc. with signposts, posted notices, guidelines, distance indicators, way marks, omens, hints, badges, stamps, emblems, ensigns, shingles". Webster

As I explore my past, I realize there were signposts along the way that I missed entirely at the time. On hindsight I see the signposts clearly. Perhaps, the exercise of examining them with a backward look will help me spot and heed them in the future. Create some mental images of sign posts. Simple references, symbols that guide and protect us when we pay attention to them. Even when we take note of them, sometimes we don't understand them unless we are willing to ask "Hey, excuse me buddy, but which way is this sign pointing?"

How often do we ignore a sign and decide we can find our own way? How desperate must we be before we admit being lost and in need of direction? How often do we refuse help when we need it, even though it is readily available? If only we would ask!

I have found these questions tough to answer honestly! Life shows me daily opportunities to broaden my bases for decision-making, and yet I have to disconnect my business-as-usual, "automatic-pilot" thinking to seek out others for their input. I know by doing so I shall gain more insights. I know other people may offer viable alternatives, maybe even much better ones! The lesson has to become part of my daily, ready-for-the-day thinking system. Too many early years of how to "behave like a man" upbringing do not get shed lightly or quickly.

I know there have been many way marks, guidelines, hints and posted notices in my life that I have sped by and ignored much to my regret.

I am reminded of one such experience of what happened when I chose to ignore the obvious signposts.

Angry Male Mail

In my second year as Headmaster of a school, my exasperation with the Board of Directors grew from simmering frustration to an explosive confrontation. From my vantage point, I had accomplished incredible things in a relatively short time. However, the Board had not picked up speed in support of my efforts. I wrote an angry letter to the Chairman of the Board itemizing what I had accomplished and what the Board had not. I wrote that unless the Board saw it my way, my resignation would be effective five months hence. The night before I mailed the letter a good friend happened to telephone to chat. I mentioned my ultimatum letter in passing. My friend was attentive and offered, "That is a strong letter. It may be too much for the Board to take."

Indignant, I ignored the first signpost, my friend's warning.

I sent the letter to the Board Chairman. He called me and acknowledged the frustration I expressed in the letter. He suggested that he would like to keep it on file and give the Board a little longer to pick up their pace.

Still insistent, I demanded the letter be forwarded to the full board disregarding the second sign, "Let's cool it for a while."

The board president reluctantly forwarded my letter to the Board and the members acted on it. The third sign board read, "You're fired." I was amazed. Of course, all of the signposts had been there, but I chose to ignore them.

It was a good lesson. I have learned to be more considerate in decision-making when I am angry or frustrated. Open feedback from a group of men like the Barn Men might have allowed me to deal with the situation more maturely and more effectively and without my smashing my head into a brick wall.

A gathering of men is helpful in sorting out boiling points and often lowering temperatures to more thought-out degrees.

Men can help other men seek and find the successful coping devices of mature adults. Trusted fellow travelers like the Barn Men can help other men grow up. Another man or youth can be listened to carefully. He can be urged not just to speak of factual details but to speak about his feelings regarding the situation. This talking "it" out, really hearing someone, non-judgmentally and accompanied by sustained eye contact does not take much training. It takes time and effort and awareness of another person who is honest enough to speak out while seeking unfettered alternatives.

Rites of passage

I call the process a "rite of passage" when a boy moves to manhood. Previous generations provided formal ceremonies to note the passage. I urge men to examine the rites of passage they have made. What sharp turns in life resulted in significant maturing changes?

Today, most men make the passage from boy to man on their own. There is no ceremony of transition overseen by elders. There are no tests for adulthood, no societal expectations of young men when they reach a certain age. Young men are dependent on themselves to make the transition from dependency on "hearth and home" to "adult" status. Adulthood in our society is often the equivalent of: a driver's license, legal drinking, entry into armed services, higher education, marriage, full-time employment, parenting, car ownership, responsibility for other peoples' welfare, life and death decisions and putting the welfare of others ahead of self. Young men rarely have "elders" to ritualistically or formally lead them out of childhood into adulthood.

A gathering of men can establish rites of passage, even for old guys who appear to be adults. A caring group of men can be empowering influences in the achievement of real maturity.

Some passages are selected. Other passages are dumped on us: the death or dying of a parent, an automobile accident, getting fired. Some passages involve a combination: planned parenthood, selecting a career, becoming a church or community leader. An integral part of each transition includes new/additional responsibilities. A gathering of men offers opportunities to speak of these transitions out of our experiences and those of our children.

Webster's Encyclopedic Unabridged Dictionary of the English Language describes a "passage hawk" as one on his first migration. Think of the hawk's initial experience of flight. Hawks follow common flyways to their destination, but they migrate independently. Canadian Geese fly together in a flock. They look out for each other, feed together, put down and arrive at their destinations together—big ones, little ones, old and young. I like the idea of the flock. I want to be affiliated.

I ask friends about their transition from childhood to manhood. Generally, their response is a confused look. "Why do you ask?" A pause and then: "Getting my driver's license, my first car, going into the armed forces, boot camp, going off to college, a serious relationship with a girl, my first 'real' job, meaningful responsibility for others, making life and death decisions." Seldom do I hear a man recall an orderly process of being guided through the passage from childhood to adulthood by an elder. Even less often have I heard a man speak of internal measures that mark the transition.

For many children of the Twentieth Century elders, fathers, uncles and grandfathers did not have a clue about leading the next generation through the process of dependent child to the front lines of adulthood. The requirements, rigors, responsibilities, plateaus on the way to adulthood were elusive. They had fallen into adult roles themselves, equally unprepared by elders. We were expected to follow suit and grow up on our own.

Restrictive role expectations for modern men do little to invite inquiry or spontaneity: get educated, go to work for forty or fifty years, make money, support a family and don't drop the ball. Personal, passionate expressions are not manly. Neither is weakness. Tough it out.

This "life script" leaves a lot of internal room for increasingly large questions as the years roll past a man. As men age, deal with increasing infirmities, meet with "brick walls", etc. concerns and worries mound up. Some men seem to encapsulate their worries and thus present a thick outer surface of only good cheer. A few others will share their worries. The rest are in a "solitary confinement" of quandary.

All men do worry about at least two things. "What sort of physical and emotional trials will I face?" And, "Can I measure up when the time comes?" We often hear these major questions simplistically expressed nowadays as, "What's happening, man?" Translate that to: "What the hell is going on, and how do I fit in or get impacted?" The "Can I measure up when the time comes?" aspect never gets asked aloud to anyone about anything! But that question is a daily, constant, lively shadow.

Mostly men do not ever speak of these veiled fears and neither did their elders. Unexpressed worry about courage on battlefields of mind or body, and fear about prevailing against heavy odds can be stifling and deplete us of energy. Our gathering of men is a safe place to speak of doubts and fears. I break the code of silence among my good friends. Practiced, I then move from the collaboration of openness in our men's group to deeper conversations outside the group without embarrassment. But it was the gathering of men that broke the taboos and let doubts and fears be expressed.

What are the questions? When do I ask them? What do I do with the answers?

Food for Thought

Who are the important people in my life? What do they bring to it? Why are they important?

When am I most authentically myself? How can I live more of my life this way?

What are my personal strengths and how do I use them to cope with the demands in my life?

What do others find worthwhile about me?

What is difficult at the present? What do I avoid? Why?

What or who provides joy in my life? How?

What do I mean by success? Failure?

What needs to be reconciled in my life?

Where, what and who are my support systems?

Who tells me I am doing a good job (in anything)?

How do I respond?

What about myself would I never abandon?

Who are my most important role models and mentors?

When I consider my life, how have I been blessed and how have I been wounded?

What have I lost, abandoned, left behind, stolen or forgotten etc. that I wish I could get back or recapture?

How did my father define faith, hope, goodness, sadness, daughter, son, wife, Jesus, sacrifice, pain, death, happiness?

How do I define these to my family?

When I pray, what do I pray about and to whom?

How have losses impacted my life?

Why do certain thoughts and events stay with me so long? Are they good or bad ones? What purpose do they serve?

What do I dream about repeatedly?

How can I get beyond persistent grieving?

What makes me cry?

How do I want to be remembered?

How do I deal with roadblocks in my life?

Probing questions are a way of gaining self-knowledge. Growing in self-awareness helps us make corrections and adjustments in life. As we engage in self-examination, we grow and reach a point where we find ourselves living effectively. Maslow calls this state being self-actualizing. We know we have reached that point in our lives when we are working to capacity and are not overextended. Our relationships are rewarding. We feel effective, creative and fulfilled. Life is not static; so as we reach one level of effectiveness, we will find new questions to address as we approach the next level of maturity. Another reason such exercises are worthwhile is that as we develop integrity in our lives we are better able to lend support and be good examples for those whom we sincerely love, and for whom we have life-long responsibility, our children to whom we have given life and children we have gained through marriage, adoption and foster parenting.

Like the ancient, Roman god, Janus, this chapter was written to help men look forward and backward. Janus gave our calendar his name for the first month of our year. Janus was the god of doorways, beginnings and of the rising and setting of the sun. His picture is of one head but with two, bearded faces. One is a young man and the other is an older man back to back looking in opposite directions. Janus gave his name to the concept of a person being "two-faced" which initially referred to someone who always saw contrasts or differences. He looked for polarities, not similarities.

Often New Years Eve or New Years Day finds people anticipating a new year with resolutions based upon events of the past. New Years is a present day use of the Janus' ideas. A person often looks backwards to determine what to do differently when looking forward. We also use the concept of looking forward and backward at the major thresholds we cross as we change occupations, change relationships, move from a familiar home to one new to us.

I can look back on my life alone or in the company of trusted Barn Men. In so doing I strengthen bonds of trust. As we learn about each other and ourselves, we grow in understanding and find affirmation in the common bonds of our manhood. This activity is a great energizer for participants as the process forms a collaborative, supportive circle of solidarity. As we "come true" in the group, we are more able to do so with wives, children and others in our lives. I think of the questioning times in our group as swimming in a community energy pool which brings renewal and personal growth at nobody else's expense.

6

Bob: Keeping the Group on Track

Choose a time and place to meet. A place where the distraction of telephones or other interruptions can be kept to a minimum. A location in a natural setting with bird songs and gentle wind sounds humming through the trees in summer establishes a relaxed environment. A wood stove in winter warms and relaxes those gathered around the fire. A central location for participants is important but it should not be the determining factor.

From our first meetings we have never paid for a meeting place. When the initial meeting place was sold, we assembled in the living room of a vacant house owned by the parents of a member. That, too, was sold. A church parish house was available for a time but there was no fire-stoking, and the room was adjacent to other frequently used rooms, so it was too public. Now we meet in a vacant gardener's office on the grounds of a member's home. The phone is turned off during meetings. The wood-burning stove adds to the room's ambience in the winter and is often the sole source of light and heat.

A room that is consistently available, at no cost is the best and is well worth looking for.

What keeps members returning is the spirit of the meeting and trust fostered by openness and sincerity.

In order to avoid absences it helps to have regularly scheduled meetings. The Barn Men meet the first and third Thursday evening of the month between 6:30 and 9:00 o'clock. Family members are aware of the commitment and note it on calendars to avoid scheduling conflicts on meeting nights.

Opening the Meeting

How do you begin? What do you do to welcome members who come in late? These are important questions to ask because setting the tone may change the texture of the meeting. We greet each other with brotherly hugs. Each man brings his own meal and informal visiting occurs during supper. At 7 o'clock each member gives a two to three minute recap of events in his life since the last gathering.

At the inception of the Barn Men we were advised to include a silence. A five-minute period of silence seemed at first to last for an eternity, but it encouraged a shift in perspective. Now unbroken silence of undetermined length goes on until someone is moved to speak. Silences have ranged from five to thirty minutes. Forget the watch.

Meet at 6:30 pm. Arrive on time; random walk-ins are disconcerting. Offer individual greetings and begin the recaps at 7 o'clock. Next, begin a period of silence. If a member has a reading to share, it should precede the silence. (Providing each member with a copy of the reading is a helpful courtesy.) Discussions follow the silence. Meetings should conclude near the agreed upon 9 o'clock.

No one is assigned to facilitate the gathering, even for an evening. Barn Men meet as equals and share responsibility. Each evening brings its own unique spirit. What happens, happens! The opening go-round eliminates the possibility of someone having something significant on his mind that goes unsaid. The go-round is a period of sharing. A three-minute hour-glass, or egg timer helps, but as a rule, members have their say before the sand runs out.

An ice-breaker "starter" can be helpful, but <u>only</u> at the first meeting. For example: "Would you tell us about your father?" Every bit of the time allotted will be used and the group will be launched.

Occasionally I have lunch with one or two members and our conversation can digress to a topic from a meeting. A bell goes off in someone's head and we agree to defer the conversation until we are all together at a meeting. We scrupulously avoid any planning outside the group. Agreeing on a topic for discussion is fine, but forming a coalition is off-limits. Many of the Barn Men have social friendships which include wives so confining Barn Men conversations to the "barn" is very important.

Meeting Glue:
What Holds The Barn Men Together?

* *Trust.* Developing a level of comfort at meetings includes the security of each member knowing he is in the company of friends. Speaking and being heard is also unifying. Listening develops empathy.

* *Must you bare your soul? No way!* There is no pressure to say one word. Of course, when you want to speak, it is fine (as long as you don't interrupt any-

one). But there is no pressure in a gathering; you do what is comfortable. If you don't want to reveal an inner thought or feeling, that is your decision.

- *Coming clean.* As the group grows in trust, it does provide an opportunity to "come clean." That is, if the group is working well, there are few barriers to honest, sometimes gut-wrenching conversation. Probing uncertainties together is a way to explore choices and is the norm in dynamic groups. Topics broach deep questions and ideas: Who am I? What do I do with my inner turmoil? How do I face the pain of my own disappointments? Why do I do the things I don't want to do and don't do the things I want? What is the purpose of my life? How will I face retirement, illness, death?

- *Confidentiality.* Confidentiality is the hallmark of a well-functioning group, and it is essential to this kind of honesty.

- *Attendance.* Regular attendance is essential for continuity and strengthening relationships of trust. Be reminded, growth occurs as a result of involvement in the group. Meetings may yield "Ah-ha!" moments as new insights are acquired. Growing spiritually, emotionally and intellectually are also attainable goals. Spotty attendance by a member signals the need to inquire. ("We have missed you and wonder how things are going for you? Is anything missing in the group that keeps you from meetings? Can we do anything to revitalize your interest?") These are direct questions which should lead to better attendance and some tips to members about what they could do to spur the absent member's interest, or it will result in the absent member removing himself from the group.)

- *Equal time.* Some groups are bogged down when one or more members dominate discussions. Someone in the group needs to ask, "Who hasn't had an opportunity to speak?" This reminds verbose speakers to share time with other less assertive members of the group who may need encouragement.

War stories

Telling stories is a way of avoiding personal sharing and undermines the goal of the group. If "war stories" begin flying around, someone needs to ask, "Why is this story important?" If the stories persist, suggest the group take time out and reenter a period of silence and reflect on what has been shared. Alternatively, direct a personal question to the tale teller, "What has been happening to you since our last meeting?"

Encouragement

Each member needs to be sensitive to the struggles of others. During our early meetings, I frequently didn't grasp the struggle a member might be trying to get off his chest until after a meeting as I reflected on what had been said. Then it was too late. If you sense a man struggling for clarity, turn up your attentive listening. Ask a simple question about what is being said: "Could you say a little more about that? What were you feeling then?"

Some of our best moments have ensued from such inquiries. In our early days one fellow shared his feelings about a dramatic sunset. No one realized he was trying to decipher a significant event in his life and the conversation turned to another topic. Later, we discovered we had lost an opportunity to lend him support during a particularly difficult time. I have always regretted it.

Blame

Humans often assign blame to others for wrongs since it is easier to recognize a failing in a person other than oneself. I don't like to admit my own flaws. The acceptance of the fact that we are, however, all flawed allows us to be kinder and to respond in love: love of self as well as the other removes the temptation of resorting to blame.

Resistance

Rome wasn't built in a day and neither is a gathering of men. Shared experiences build relationships. Trust grows. "I" messages and the absence of advice or assignments of blame are in the featherbed of trust. Such environments are comfortable and overcome resistance to openness.

As groups mature, a member can seize an opportunity that might previously have been glossed over. A thoughtfully couched question can unearth feelings and turn conversations in helpful directions.

Confidence

There is a direct relationship between trust and a willingness to openly share our essence. The quality of a gathering is proportional to each man's commitment to keep conversations in the "barn". When asked by a family member, "How was your meeting?" the standard reply is, "Our meetings are usually meaningful." Or a similar comment is shared. Should there be a breach of confidentiality, it needs to be discussed at a meeting with all members present.

To err is human. To face this truth and talk it out is the only way to resolve such a breach of trust. Rebuilding trust will take time, but it can happen if all wish it to be. Some violations of trust will necessitate the removal of the member. This is a question the membership will have to address and decide together.

Advice

Sharing personal experience is helpful but offering advice is discouraged. Advice changes dialogue from peer-sharing to a teacher-student orientation. If, in response, a man speaks of the way he handled a similar predicament, it can be helpful. However, what served a third party in a similar situation takes the dialogue "out of the barn."

One liners

Sarcasm and honesty don't mix. It means it's time for a check-in to uncover the source of hurtful comments and put an end to them.

Journals

Journaling is useful in gaining personal clarity via a conversation with an objective "bird on your shoulder." Several introductions to the methods of journaling are found in Natalie Goldberg's, *Writing Down the Bones* and Ira Progoff's, *At a Journal Workshop.* Seeing your thoughts on paper can be helpful in discovering points for discussion at meetings.

Observer to Participant

Creative listening is good to a point, but a functional group needs everyone to listen, speak, participate and dialogue. This is hard for some, easy for others but essential to a successful group.

Anger

Anger, expressed in an appropriate way, is healthy, life-giving and cleansing. Anger toward another man in the group can erupt. Working out the anger, then and there, develops a template for dealing with it effectively whenever it creeps in.

Reflections

Think of times you have met with a group. What added to the experience? What would have improved it? A personality assessing indicator is a useful means of learning to know yourself as you prepare to join a self-discovery group.

"I" messages

These are the three levels of communication: "I must talk about, I ought to, and I am...." Have meetings that move toward the third. Learning to speak from the "I" position is important. This communication skill is a transforming element of an effective group. When using "I," a man speaks for himself and no other. When I speak from my experience and not on behalf of any or all other men, I deliver a personal message. "We," "you" or "one," creates a distance. Of all meeting guidelines this may be the most important and most difficult to put into practice.

Can an occasional guest be helpful? Yes, absolutely. The Barn Men have met with a nun, two women approaching their nineties, and a man who is in a gathering of men in Massachusetts. The woman who helped us as we started the Barn Men attended a meeting several years later. Guests offer new insights and fresh ways of looking at life.

Is any topic off limits? No, but general, theoretical or philosophical expositions can be distractions from specific concerns.

Is the group a sanctuary? I guess so, but I have never heard a Barn Man describe our group that way. Just as rarely have I heard a wooded glen described as a cathedral, but it is to me.

7

Derek: Living in the Present

Richard J. Leider writes in, *It's the Time of Your Life:* "Mountains have always drawn people to them, wherever they are. The mountain quest is an age-old metaphor. When I step into a wilderness or onto a mountain, there is an eternal mystery which is one of its most compelling attractions for me."

"Great things are done when men and mountains meet; this is not done by jostling in the street." William Blake in *Gnomic Verses.*

When Richard Leider, speaker, author and editor of *The On Purpose Journal* reached his fiftieth birthday, he realized, "Time is a gift and there is no such thing as 'free' time." To drive the point home to himself, to his readers and to his audiences he purchased a Life-Clock. It was set for him alone and it measures the hours and minutes remaining in his statistical lifetime.

Each year Richard Leider begins by creating his "Life Map" for the year ahead. His mantra, "Nothing shapes our lives as much as the questions we ask-or refuse to ask."

Then he asks himself, "What do I want to do?" and "What's stopping me from doing it?" He writes, "Every person eventually faces a quest, a time when he or she is challenged to define his or her time on this planet. An 'inventure quest' begins when we turn away from our standard answers and look toward bigger questions…The challenge…is being responsible for stepping from the land of 'I know' to the land of 'I don't know.' Real change means you'll need a real plan. A real plan takes courage, letting go, climbing one step at a time, even if you are terrified."

The paths the Barn Men have taken have brought each man, just as it has Richard Leider, to a place in life where honesty and integrity are sought and realized through major life changes. Each man joined at a different age; some in their fifties, others in their sixties or seventies and one at eighty.

"Mid-life crises" were not the catalysts for membership as one skeptic suggested when he heard of the Barn Men. Invigorating, personal growth is the launch pad. We all joined seeking more out of life. Barn Men seek to live more fully, more deeply, more broadly, more honestly and to be more spiritually in tune. Meetings are not held in a fiery furnace where men are forged or broken. The meetings are safe places in which to ask "growth edge" questions. Thoughtful, personal questions that inspire or elicit inquiries from others are gems in meetings. They really stimulate reflective thinking.

Mountains are the metaphor of our mutual adventure and we are all over the mountain. Some are wandering among the foothills. Others have ascended one summit after another throughout their lives. They have embraced change, grown in countless ways and, like Robert Frost, have chosen less frequently traveled paths. Individual quests extend from the hub of our selves—from our core like the spokes of a wheel. One spoke represents faith; another, prayer; yet another religious affiliation.

Spiritual legacies and ideas for children and grandchildren occupy another spoke. We are reminded of medicine wheels, wheels which connect us with others. Balancing our life wheels can improve our lives by rounding off rough edges. Personal growth occurs in our fellowship as we gather ideas and unfold them on the table around which we meet as Barn Men. The dynamics of such experiences are like personal spiritual growth wheels. As the wheels turn, we discover we have expanded our thinking at the same time as we have deepened the quality of our fellowship with others. A non-member's story illuminates ways personal growth experiences cut across cultural and geographic boundaries and occur in groups or individually.

A Non-Member's Story: Vision Quest

Peter has packed many experiences into his fifty years. Long, dark curly hair tumbles over the weathered face of this compact, wiry man who exudes energy. He hates to sit still. When engaged in conversation with Peter, you realize he will tackle any topic. The easy flow of conversation with Peter is sustained by his intense interest in practically everything.

During a conversation about highlights in our lives since we last visited the year before, Peter sat engraving an antique firearm in preparation for an upcoming art show. I mentioned I was co-authoring a book about the Barn Men and told him about our group. As I explained the group's purpose of self-discovery and growth, he grew increasingly thoughtful: "Like what?" he asked.

I told him we examined our spiritual lives, "Have you examined your spiritual life, Peter?" I asked. Peter stopped working with his engraving tools and gave undivided attention to his thoughts as he dredged deep inside himself and then said:

I was born and reared in East Germany. My father was a Protestant and my mother a Roman Catholic; therefore, I was brought up Catholic. I remember it was a big amount of work—much rote memory, to prepare for confirmation in the church. When the time came, it was a big deal. I fully expected a major Epiphany to happen to me right there and then. But nothing happened. I was no different. I felt nothing different. It was a total let down. I ceased believing everything I had spent so many hours learning. The Eucharist held no meaning for me whatsoever. I thought over and over about the gift of flesh and blood and it held no meaning for me. I abandoned my faith. A few years later, I escaped from East Germany and fled west. Eventually, I landed in Düsseldorf, I married, had a child and almost 'went nuts' in the advertising business. I was so 'successful' that each day I started with a shot or two of whiskey just to jolt myself into the crazy race in which I was immersed. Then all of the dazzle fell apart. I was fired, divorced, and estranged from my child. It was a fast trip from top to bottom. Once again, I was moving west. I arrived at an Indian Reservation with nothing. I had no books, job, family or religion but a Hopi friend said I was welcome to stay. I was left to myself and ignored by the general community. It was a bad, bad time in my life. I brooded. After considerable time another Hopi friend visited me and said it was time to climb the mountain on a 'vision quest.' It was time for me to take responsibility for living. I had a life and I was wasting it.

"Go," he said and, "take water, but no food; go by yourself and pray."

"Pray to whom or what?" I asked.

*"Pray to whomever or whatever listens. Do not expect an immediate response."
My friend said, "Take a gift." I had nothing but the filthy clothes on my dirty body. It was obvious to my Hopi friend and to me I needed to find my way in life so I went to the mountain. I took an arrowhead for some reason. I guess it was all that I really 'owned.' I climbed to the summit of the mountain, stayed, prayed and endured. I longed for something to happen to understand what life had for me. Nothing happened, except misery. I was cold, hungry, alone. Then something began to happen. I sensed the presence of spirits around me. My vision appeared. I had the personal vision I had anticipated so many years before and awoke to the meaning of my life.*

I had it. The time in Düsseldorf spent looking for rewards of money and possessions brought me nothing by way of satisfaction, and in trying to hang onto what I accumulated I lost it all—along with everyone I cared for. Acquisitions afford no lasting satisfaction. At the same moment, I realized idly, sitting by myself wondering what was in it for me was a waste of time. Finally, I grasped life's meaning. My life belonged to me. I had it. Life was a gift. It was mine to give, to pour out for others, and I have done so.

I recognized my life is to use. The only possession I need is mine—myself, my talent. I understood my gift.

Gifts aren't to save; they are to share. Life is to share, and I was, at last, pre-pared to do it. In gratitude for the revelation of the spirits, "the vision", I took the arrowhead from my pocket and cut my arm as a thank offering to the spirits. It was the only gift I could offer—my blood—myself.

My life would redeem no one, but I could offer the gift of my life and I learned to do so.

Turning to me, Peter told me, "Look, I have a life, a wife; I am reconciled with my children. I have it all." Peter gestured around the gallery which included the exquisite works of art he had created, an intricately-engraved Navy revolver, a glimmering knife and sheath, an oil painting of a mesa revered by the Hopi, beautifully worked silver jewelry. All crafted by this deeply thoughtful, passionate man. Peter was pouring out his gifts for the enjoyment of others and he had never known more peace or joy.

Peter needed quiet time to emerge from recalling his profound experience. As he departed from childish expectations of getting something out of life and matured, he freely gave himself. And in so doing, he received life's real treasures, the gift of integrity, joy, love and peace.

Peter is not a member of the Barn Men, but his story is a beautiful example of what Barn Men seek as they approach the mountain top. Peter's story left both of us emotionally spent. His honesty gave our friendship new meaning.

As Barn Men encounter the paradox of the Golden Rule they find fodder for meetings. Do unto others as you would have them do unto you…love God, neighbor and self. Splendid, high-minded admonitions juxtaposed against caveats to, "Take care of yourself first because nobody else will. Think of Number One. Don't get mad, get even." Our response to these admonitions is tested daily, if not hourly. We learn that life is not a simple push/pull equation.

Getting Something for Your Quarter

In the days of my elementary education, school lunches in New York City were regarded as not particularly edible or pleasing. Consequently, some of us would sidle out of the lunchroom and scamper three blocks down to the place of "real" lunches, the Automat. As you fingered your collection of shiny quarters, you were faced with bank after bank of small, highly polished chromium doors surround-ing clear glass. Through the glass you could see a vast variety of sandwiches, sal-ads, pies, cakes, hot and cold delights. Each door had a slot where you inserted a quarter and then pulled a handle to raise the door and retrieve the item on dis-play. You put your quarter in and out came the exact sandwich you expected. It happened every time. At the Automat life was the ultimate of "quid pro quo".

You put your quarter in and instantly you got back an equal value sandwich. Simple.

Random Acts of Kindness and the Golden Rule

Real life teaches that if you do some out-of-the-way courtesy for a stranger, or even for an acquaintance, you should not expect a return on your kindness. As mature adults we put aside the formulaic days of the Automat. Much of the time there is no acknowledgement of the good turns we do. We may attempt to give the rarest of all attributes, gratitude, to others but we will be disappointed if we expect to find it waiting for us.

Living in a society with people who may or may not share my beliefs takes some figuring out.

As someone who tries to operate in the practical school of "what works," I discover my purposes are better-served when I do not base decisions on expectations of someone else. Not assigning expectations to others allows me to act on the tenets I hold true.

I want to act on the Golden Rule regardless of the response. This decision is easier to keep when there is a supportive fellowship to reinforce my decision of charity over cruelty or charity without appreciation. The Barn Men discuss the fractures and fragments that are the consequences of The Golden Rule and we support one another in upholding it.

We identify our personal fears, anger, love and purpose in order to refine our value system. Examining value judgments in a group is a means of acquiring empathy. Values, not cast in stone, are flexible and dynamic and don't sleep much.

The values of others can shade our own unconsidered values until we clarify our beliefs. We say, "Hold it! That is not my way of doing things or thinking things. What am I thinking? What am I doing?" I would suggest that real friends can step in at this point. If my behavior is heading me into a large brick wall, I want a friend to alert me to my trajectory and the harsh reality of impending impact.

One of the benefits of being a Barn Man is the development of large, strong bridges of trust which allow a fellow member to utilize that bridge to cry out and not fear rejection. What does it mean to be thoughtful of one's fellows? What does concern mean for a friend? What is our group wittingly striving for? How do we look out for each other and still others?

It is all fine and dandy to talk about high-minded ideas, but acting out our high-minded beliefs is the real test of where we operate. As we strive for healthy actions—and reactions—we look for positive role models. Barn Men searches bring us to new, more thoughtful feelings and interactions in widening circles of interesting people. We learn daily that we are not in control of our lives, only our responses. Internal events like discovering cancer residing within us or external events like the death of a child lead us to understand we have limited control. The challenge is how we will cope with events, devastating or otherwise.

Four members of the Barn Men have been diagnosed with cancer. The group has provided an incredible forum for sharing the aftermath of the diagnoses. Each man's experience has been openly shared. A simple observation by one cancer infested man was the "life raft" for others. He said of his treatment journey, "I just keep myself afloat." The conviction of the speaker and his statement became a lifeline for others so afflicted. We cannot move forward unless we face our fantasies and our facts with a plan, and with confidence.

Being reminded of our mission to stay afloat in a rudderless state reinforces our determination. Checking in with each other between meetings is strengthening.

How does "loving God, neighbor and self" fit in? We have choices for our reactions to life. When we acknowledge the missing aspects of our lives, we can make changes and better choices. Change is very scary for many of us because it is a leap into the unknown. It requires faith to jump between the known and unknown. We must make a commitment to move in a new direction. When a person looks to the mountain top, he sees a goal and puts himself on a path with *clear purpose* as a companion. As clear purpose emerges, an emboldened sense of self-worth ignites a spark which can grow into an internal flame and encourage our hearts and minds to "go for it" with gusto.

We realize such purpose is worthy and honorable. Love of fellow man enables the climber to find and embrace companions who will aid and abet each other openly and honestly. Friendship is not status quo. It requires the energy of mutual renewal. Love is a bond that develops between friends.

So as Richard Leider wisely observed, the "mountains" we climb in life, be they granite peaks or the foothill challenges of daily living, can, with honest effort, lead to the peaks where mankind interacts knowingly with the divine. During the ascent a climber realizes there is much to leave behind. Grudges are no good. Grabbing the spotlight for oneself at any cost is no good. The climber will also recognize the divine spark in each individual and gain an entirely new perspective on the people he chances upon.

He will recognize not only frailties and foibles in others, but strengths as well. This positive outreach toward others generates love for one's fellow man as well as for our selves. This is a quest for community, and one that unites mankind. Living the Golden Rule on the mountain peak rather than remaining in the confounding valley of paradoxes is the aim of the Barn Men. As we older fellows grow in wisdom, we can guide and lead our sons and their sons.

We can walk with confidence with younger men and prepare them for adulthood—firm in the conviction that wise men are loving, human beings. That done, we can be somewhat more secure in the aspiration that we have tried to leave succeeding generations in more qualified hands.

8

Bob: The Meaning of Silence

"It's taken me a long time to learn that being alone is not loneliness. I now cherish my time alone. It can occur outside, walking through the woods, or standing by the water. But if I am not in some kind of community, then time alone doesn't work as well." Michael Meade, *On Being a Man, An Interview with Michael Meade* by Sy Safransky: *The Sun Newspaper.*

Interiorscape

"Our real journey in life is interior: it is a matter of growth, deepening and ever greater surrender to the creative action of love and grace in our hearts." Merton, Thomas. *The Asian Journal of Thomas Merton*, edited from his original notebooks by, Naomi Burton, Brother Patrick Hart, and James Laughlin. New York: New Directions Books, 1968.

Silence

Silence in a gathering of men offers a profound opportunity today. Silence is important in Western culture, so filled with noise and external stimulation. Continual workplace chatter, television and countless noisy distractions rob us of time to examine the truth of our lives. How can life be examined without silence? Silence is my opportunity to experience what Thomas Berry refers to as "the vast web of interrelations that exist between all natural phenomena." Berry adds, "We understand the flow of energy whereby each reality sustains and is sustained by all the other realities of the entire world."

In Berry's search for meaning, he attempted to answer three questions: "Where are we? How did we get here? and What do we do about it?" He suggests, "In its every aspect, the human is a participatory reality. We are members of the great universe community. We participate in this life. We are nourished by this community, we are instructed by this community, we are healed by this community. In and through this community, we enter into communion with that luminous mystery whence all things depend for their existence and their activity." Probing the depths of silence is an essential step on the journey of life.

Gaining Confidence with Silence

Our experience of silence together has become one of the principal incentives for attendance.

Each silence is different. Some "work" better than others—it depends on where you are and how you settle into it. The intent is to let go of the day's issues and "get to the other side" or "to another plane."

There is no formula for this! Still your mind and let whatever will form, bubble up. It is a letting go. A thought will come and then disappear. Another will stick around to be related to the others when dialogue resumes.

Often, it helps to close your eyes and still your focus. Some find placing their hands on their knees with the palms up invites new thoughts. I find my limited experience with Yoga helps; I focus on a muscle in my face or neck and if it is tight, I try to let it go and relax it. My foot or leg might be tight, so I draw it in tighter—then let it go.

Sometimes it is like cutting the lawn, or like times the music gets stuck on a continually repeating track. My mind goes round and round on the same theme. This happens when my mind isn't stilled and I haven't let go of the day's activities.

During some silences I wonder what the other men are feeling and thinking and it is difficult to turn within myself. That's a good sign of wanting to listen to others. I remember a long silence at one meeting broken by a question, "What is going on for you?" This led to a rich sharing.

Breaking a Silence

Since the Barn Men have no leader or facilitator, each man has a responsibility—not to do anything in particular but to remain open and avoid passivity. Sometimes during a silence there may be something I feel like sharing. And I give myself permission to talk. It's not calculated, written down or in any way "organized." Nor is it premeditated on the way to the meeting or during the days before the meeting. I start sharing what is on my mind right now. This might take a minute, or as many as five minutes. Occasionally, a challenging issue may lead a man to speak longer. That is fine and it is agreed that while he speaks, no one will interrupt him. Also, no one asks questions. No one gives advice. The purpose of each man's outpouring is to share from within himself. It is essential not to slide into stories outside the present moment (see "war stories" in Chapter Six).

Approaching "The Dead Moose on the Table"

Meeting facilitators use the saying "dead moose on the table" to suggest situations that include difficult issues no one mentions. They describe it as, "A large, stinky moose sitting on the table and never discussed despite its stinking in front of all present!" Silence in a gathering of men is a technique to eliminate the possibility of "a stinking moose" being denied and avoided.

A climate to address the dead moose is encouraged when we quietly face our thoughts and let them out if they are relevant. How different this setting is from the usual closed environments. Trusting that the Barn Men will lovingly accept whatever I say helps me face my *dead mooses*.

Over time, as I have learned of other men's challenges, I am aware that much of what swims under the surface of each man's life has a common thread. This was a powerful insight and its byproduct is an increased personal willingness to face, confront and let go.

On the other hand, sometimes a member will remain quiet for most of a meeting. Before the meeting ends, it can be helpful to inquire how he is doing. This often helps him break a "log jam" and leads to insightful sharing that closes a meeting.

Five Steps of Prayer

There are five parts of prayer: praise, thanksgiving, contrition, intercession, and petition. They are useful to know in keeping silence. Bringing them to silence can increase the dimensions of silence. Recognizing God or the Ultimate Energy of life on Earth and offering Him praise puts life in context. Offering gratitude and thanks for what I have received, through no effort of my own, is important. Giving my mind to what I want for others, my community, my country, or the world, is imperative. Recognizing what I regret and could have done better lead me to new ways of living. And, finally intercession on someone's behalf, or petitions on my own behalf, help me access my circumstances and goals.

The Ultimate Energy, Eternal Spirit

Each Barn Man's expression of his connection or carefully-considered lack of connection to God is respected by the others. Some regard God as Ultimate Energy, Higher Power, Eternal Spirit, Earth Maker, Pain Bearer, and/or Life

Giver. Allah, Jehovah, or the Triune God, Father, Son and Holy Spirit. Still others have and share other views about their spiritual beliefs. Each acknowledges something beyond human understanding, using whatever words define the undefineable. A reflection offered during a Barn Men evening suggests the power of prayer. Jim Simmons framed it like this: "Prayer puts us in a position for that of God within us to emerge."

Differing Silences

Silence in a gathering of men can be different from silences done solo or in retreats. Solo silences sometimes occur when the music is turned off, but such silences are different because they don't allow for a bubbling up of thoughts and feelings. They are task-oriented.

Retreats of church groups and others are directed and may include a leader. These can last several days or more and can be enhanced by keeping a journal. This experience can be profound and contribute to the silence with a gathering of men. Inquire at a church or a nearby retreat center that others have attended. Learn about the various options and formats. Usually they are for one or more overnights. Not all retreats are done in silence.

When the Barn Men meeting goes into silence, the group's collective energy is obvious. The men are working, their wheels are turning, yet the only sound is quiet breathing. Each man is digging, but there is no expression, no result, or even evidence of anything happening. No one has an assignment or an agenda—everyone is working in his immediate now. I have no other time in my life that is like this. Is it scary? Absolutely. Is it challenging? Yes. But in these reflective moments occasionally the "luminous mystery" can be plumbed. When a silence works for me, it breaks with issues of my day and takes me to a deeper, quieter place.

Other Kinds of Silence

There is a silence unrelated to the silence desired by a gathering of men. Some keep quiet to hide from others, or to block others' desire to control or gain something. Forcing someone to keep silent is oppressive.

An introvert is more accustomed to going within than an extrovert who is outwardly oriented. Using silence is a learned skill developed with practice. The more silence is experienced and the various approaches to silence are employed, the more likely one is to find a rewarding and productive result.

Silence in one venue can lead to effective silence in other venues. Sometimes stopping to quietly observe others, leads to new insights or heightened awareness.

Practicing silence at home is good. In the car, my best time to observe silence is on my drive to work. The drive after work might not be so productive since my mind is racing over the day's events. I can observe silence on a walk, too.

Awaking in the early morning with 3 o'clock issues and worries is not the same kind of silence and this type presents different challenges. When this happens, I take a "pee break" and if I don't get back to sleep, I recite a favorite prayer or a poem or, if all else fails, count sheep.

Peace from Silence

When entering silence, forget your watch. The length of time is not the issue. A rule for the Barn Men is that during meetings any member may spontaneously ask for a "time out" for silence. When it is requested, it is often because discussions are moving too quickly from one topic to another leaving little or no time for reflection between topics. We appreciate a period of time after one man speaks before another takes the floor. This allows time for reflection.

Letting Silence Work for You

In a silence, you don't prescribe what happens. What happens, happens. You let go, still your mind, listen and feel, especially in your gut and in your muscles. Silence allows for new, unexpected experiences that add to greater understanding of self and the world. Give it a go!

For me, silence varies with each experience. Sometimes it is flat. During other sessions, I have become stuck on one thought. Sometimes I am the one to break the evening's silence. At other times I can travel down or up to new realizations. Each time I need to experience it anew and see what happens. I try to let it be a surprise. And each meeting I am thankful for the experience of silence.

9

Derek: On Listening

"His listening allowed me to develop my thoughts. While I talked, his eyes never wandered. He looked directly at me and gave me his full attention as if nothing else mattered in that moment. The more he listened, the more I was able to express myself and the more certain I became about what I was saying. This experience taught me a great deal about the power of listening, about how fundamentally important it is in helping leaders dream and form their visions of the future...."

"Sit in a council circle. Select a favorite item as a 'talking stick'. Pass it clockwise around the circle. Each person is asked to speak *leanly* from the heart when he holds the stick. The others listen deeply, with respect as the speaker shares his views. Speaking without planning ahead allows each person to listen completely until it is his/her turn. By sitting in a circle each person realizes an equity and shared value in the ideas expressed."

Joseph Jaworski in, *64 Ways to Practice Nonviolence* written and edited by Eisha Mason and Peggy DoBreer.

Here are some questions and additional commentary related to the topic of listening from the same source:

What is the difference between hearing something and listening to something?

Who really listens to you? Whom do you really listen to?

How does it change your feeling about someone when you know you have been heard and understood?

Do you listen with your ears, or your heart?

"Today, stop what you are doing and take five minutes to listen to the feelings beneath someone's words. Be fully present for the conversation and be interested in what the person is feeling and saying."

In election years, radio and television sets blast messages that are largely ignored by listeners who have become immune to them. Night after night, day after day shouting matches interrupted by loud, paid advertising fall on deaf ears. Endless partisan monologues sometimes aired with gruesome visuals confound audiences. Viewers cannot follow the babble which is supposed to entertain but instead confuses and annoys. After these assaults on eyes and ears, attending a gathering of men is like entering a sanctuary.

The frenetic pace is left outside the door. Attendees do not talk over each other. Sidebar conversations are infrequent and discouraged. Genuine attentive listening is the goal of the group and it rejuvenates the body and soul.

Attentive listening is the acquired skill, and it is necessary to really hear a message. As I reflect on my childhood, I recall sitting, raptly listening to stories my grandfather told of wilderness experiences deep in the Canadian woods. He spoke of building emergency fires to keep wolves at bay as he waited in the semi-darkness of evening for the arrival of the canoe bearing his rendezvous guide. As he spoke I could see the dancing flames and the wolves' eyes leering from the untamed forest. I remained spellbound for a minute or two after the story ended, savoring each word.

His story created vivid mental images. I was thrilled with each retelling of the story because he would slip in more details and I could experience the story once again.

On summer nights when I was a boy, my cousins and I gathered on blankets in a hayfield in front of my grandfather's house which overlooked the White Mountains of New Hampshire and we told ghost stories. At the beginning of the evening, there was room to spare between each child. An aunt or uncle would start the story. Stars sparkled in the darkness and shooting stars were silently wished upon. As the stories unfolded, grisly detail by detail, the children inched closer and closer to one another. It was not only the chill of evening that drew us close but also the vivid images of the scary stories.

One night as the story tellers instilled heaping portions of fear in the group, and we children were packed like sardines, there was a terrifying noise, compounded by the sound of heavy hoof beats. What ghastly tale was being made manifest in our midst?

None.

The neighbor's cows had escaped the rickety fencing and been quietly enjoying the lush uncut hay field. As they made their way through the dark field and came upon the mound of people, they fled in fright.

There was very little honor among children or adults as we also made a hasty retreat from the field. Cows and people fled every which way shrieking and bellowing. When we were secure at the top of the wide porch steps, the panic subsided. The first to regain his breath spoke of the fearsome marauders. Everyone assembled again, snuggling closer, to hear jumbled accounts of the incident. As we grasped what had happened, a collective giggle overtook the human herd as we realized we were safe, sound and slightly silly.

Years have passed, but our family still loves to retell various versions of the same, old, wild cow story. Before television and radio precluded such gatherings, we listened to one another and thoroughly enjoyed story telling. Being together to speak and be heard was a great source of pleasure.

An article in a September, 2002 *Parade Magazine* by Dr. Joyce Brothers caught my attention. A caveat of the Barn Men is to avoid the, "You shoulds…" If someone slips into the "shoulds," we remind the offender, "Don't should on me and I won't should on you".

Listening is a far cry from telling another what he or she should do. After I read and reread Dr. Brothers' brief article, I embellished her suggestions with observations of my own acquired by facilitating leadership seminars for business people and students. I put the combined ideas onto four by six inch cards and entitled the top card, *LISTENING.* I put the cards beside the kitchen telephone to use during conversations. Their proximity to the kitchen table where spontaneous conversations sprout wings is also helpful.

Nitty-gritty of the cards

"Listen with mind and body. Be 'engaged' in a conversation. Focus on where the speaker 'is' and not on a goal. Listen. Don't frame replies as the other person speaks. Ask questions to clarify ideas and feelings. Listen to the whole story. What are the relationships of the people involved? Peel back the layers of a message three or five levels with sequential questioning.

Ask of the speaker:

What does he want to do?

How is he moving toward a solution?

Does he want support only?

Does he want only to "ventilate."

Just listening may be all that the speaker wants. Action is not always needed. Clarify what needs "fixing."

Ask:

What would you like to change?
What would you like to accomplish?
Ask the speaker for a restatement.
Reframe the statements of what you heard as a listener and ask: Did I hear you say _____?

Let the speaker clarify his statement(s). Write down the speaker's clarified statements. Help the speaker develop options.
Ask:
What action steps come to your mind?
What do you think might achieve your goals?
What might the results of the options be?
How will the actions impact you, the speaker?
How will your action plan impact others?

Keep in mind the power of a listener. Appreciate and recognize the trust involved. Consider whether the listener should give opinions, if directly asked. Assess your own biases before responding. Be the "objective listener."

Qualify any response as representative of the listener's values system and experiences. Never suggest to the speaker that which cannot be changed. Consider what the listener is getting out of being the listener in this situation.

Remember that the listener cannot be helpful if not as honestly objective as possible. If the problem exceeds your experience or expertise or is very serious, help the speaker find a qualified person to help.

One way we practice hearing and listening among the Barn Men is by using the questions Lew Mills prepared to dialogue with his son (see end of this chapter). They are cited time and again in meetings and have inspired others outside our group. I suggest open-ended questions. In our family setting it is an approach that is helpful in thinking through problems. We can ponder responses for a day or two before responding. Quick responses are deliberately avoided. The question is not a "gotcha" question, but a question posed in a way as to remove the layers beneath an idea to get closer to the core of the situation. Questions asked in this fashion let the speaker know an ongoing awareness and concern is available. There are ears to hear when the speaker is ready.

The authors use the expression, "unpacking someone" and "peeling back the layers". These expressions signify that someone is "full to bursting" with feelings about a situation, good or bad, and he needs someone to listen to him and acknowledge what we call "information spills."

This is not like a dental extraction; it is meant as a kind, thoughtful, trusting means to let people speak from the heart. We have "unpacked" them when they "peel back the layers" of the problem to the core. The listener has the dual role of questioner also.

"Unpeeling" is a different process. What is meant here is to size up a situation and ask questions. The first responses tend to be superficial or safe responses. The questioner continues asking more questions related to the previous response until asking a question that elicits the toughest answers: Why did such and such happen? What is the real issue behind all this? The "whys" are often tough to answer because they get to the insides of the speaker who must fully trust the listener with the heart of the matter. It is a difficult search for truth, but this search will often set us free.

In my experience, conversations, do indeed, go on at home between husband and wife, parent and child, grandparents, children and grandchildren, in-laws and their counterparts, friends and neighbors and associates at work. By sharing thoughts and feelings, fears and joys at meetings, others beyond the meetings benefit. As we share knotty issues within our Barn Men fellowship, we receive valuable responses which are non-judgmental. Insights are gained from unbiased dialogue.

For instance, if I hit a communication rut with a grandchild I want to guide during a difficult decision-making process, I am glad to know that by sharing my dilemma with Barn Men I may find my way across the rut. When I mention being stymied during a Barn Men meeting, another Barn Man may offer, "Oh, I have been there, too. What got us out of our pickle was _____." He has not said, "Well, you should do the following." He recognizes my dilemma and helps me see a new path to the desired destination. I value the input, and it often takes me beyond "boxed in" thinking.

There is another aspect of listening. The foregoing has focused on listening to sources from outside self. Barn Men recognize and believe in attending to their own inner voices.

Listening and hearing skills are learned over many years. As outward hearing grows fainter, strength from inner hearing carries me forward and fine-tunes my awareness of life and death.

Lew's Questions for His Son

What do you like about me? What don't you like?

How could I have been a better father?

What do you need from me now that you are a grown man?
What would you like to tell me about yourself?
What more would you like to know about me?
Where/how have I failed you most?
What thrilled you as a youngster?
What hurt the most growing up?
How do you want to be remembered?
What would you have me change?
What would you tell a friend about me?
When I tell you I love you, what happens to you?

Sensitive (and not overwhelming) use of the above is advised.

10

Derek: Measures of Success

When measuring the success of a men's group, attendance is a key. Unless a member is out of town or quite sick, every effort to attend meetings is made. Travel to meetings requiring an hour each way on good evenings, or inclement weather, are not impediments to attendance in successful groups. During the course of a meeting, everyone contributes to the conversation in some way. Occasionally, a member who is unusually quiet is drawn out by gentle questioning.

Other gauges include the introduction of substantive, honest feelings and ideas into meetings. Individuals leave feeling better for having attended. When individuals and the group have dialogue on challenges such as death, disease, personal anxieties, family sufferings, work stress, increasing age and spiritual growth, it is safe to conclude the meetings are successful. Highly developed listening skills are markers in successful meetings. Empathy toward one another is evident. Acknowledgment that the group has a positive influence is an indicator of success. Improved patterns of expression and communication are observable. An environment lacking in competitive elements is apparent. Open sharing is the standard. Fear of scorn or criticism is nonexistent.

Concern translates as love when a group supplies unqualified support to one another. Mutual support among the members is not based on typical relationships such as husband/wife, father/child, and employee/employer. This is a group of laymen living in the real world of avarice, greed, "road-rage" and self-centeredness, but defensive barriers are not in attendance.

This sounds fine and dandy, but a skeptic may ask for specific examples of integrating words and actions.

A typical Barn Men meeting holds many examples of why we choose to put aside tugs and pulls of other commitments to spend a few hours in fellowship twice a month.

A Typical Meeting

Note: It was the consensus of the Barn Men to leave their names attached to the anec-
dotal stories that follow. These substantiate the Barn Men's commitment to speak the
truth in love and thus reveal aspects of their identities.

Once the Barn Men were established in their meetings, there were obvious
signs of contentment at being together. Hugs among members were offered with
sincerity. The fire in the stove warmed the people and the room.

In one meeting Jim had arrived early and started the fire in the ancient wood
stove. When thanked, he demurred, saying he enjoyed arriving half an hour early,
making and starting the fire. He said feeling the heat chased away the cold, damp
lingering winter and he was relishing the peace and quiet as the fire slowly crack-
led to life. It was rewarding.

We all enjoy the confusion and jostling as the group assembles. Some men sit
in the same spot at each meeting; others follow up a greeting and seek a seat near
the conversationalist. Home-made and store-bought dinners are laid on the table;
chips and starter foods are shared as tempting scents of the meals intermingle.
Someone brings out the three-minute timer and plops it in front of a seatmate
with the admonishment. "Go ahead and start, Joe, since you are mostly through
chewing."

Joe gives an account of his step-daughter's struggle with a consuming cancer.
His heavy burden is ever so slightly lifted as he shares it. The next speaker
expresses his pleasure that his work in oil and watercolors is progressing to his satisfaction. He says he is glad to be accomplishing good work and enjoys a sem-
blance of order in his life. And so around the table we follow the three-minute
glass. A member is permitted to pass the timer without speaking if he wants to,
but before the silence begins, we return the timer to him and ask him to bring a
part of his life to the group.

In one such meeting silence settled after the last man spoke. It was almost
immediately broken by Jack who remarks that he will really miss Hal who has
retired from the Barn Men just short of his eighty-ninth year. Others agree with
nods and warm words. We return to silence.

After another silence of about fifteen minutes, Carter breaks in with one of his
usual gems. He has brought up one particular topic before, at other meetings, but
it always surfaced toward the end of the meeting when time did not permit
addressing it. This time it's a good opener. Carter's concern is that in the past as
he entered a new decade, he looked forward to something positive happening in
the upcoming ten-year-period. Now as he approaches his seventh decade, he has

nothing on the horizon to look forward to with anticipation. "Do any of you feel this way, or is it just me? He asks, "Is this a fork in the road where I choose between being a kindly or a grumpy old man?"

"Is our attitude a choice?" inquires one man.

"What I wonder," responds Carter, "is, do people decide how they are going to be, at a certain age?

For instance, Derek has spoken lovingly of his grandfather's helping him through his teenage years by taking him on fishing trips to Canada and working side by side in his rose gardens; of how his grandfather was such a thoughtful, caring, wise mentor for him. Other men have spoken about the difficulties of dealing with irascible, petulant, negative older people, including their own, and their spouse's parents. Do older people choose to become mean-spirited as they enter their concluding decades?

One asks, "What is ahead for me?" This launches a lengthy dialogue of interest to every man in the room.

How will we behave as we age, grow less sturdy, change self-image, be unable to do things we are accustomed to doing? Each man expresses his concerns without interruption. We listen with heart and mind and each of us mulls aging and shares whatever he is thinking without fear of contradiction, or putdown. In fact, he is sincerely encouraged to formulate his ideas. "Idea spills," such as these, have feelings attached to them. So we explore the attendant feelings. I speak of my fears openly. I hear the fears of others and we sort out our feelings together.

In a gathering of men we openly accept and affirm each other. We learn to face our fears and seek wisdom in the community of our fellowship. We know that to show our sons better ways of engaging, grappling and growing through similar experiences, will require wisdom and choosing to look squarely at the truth. Maybe being kindly old men is a choice. Our question then becomes <u>how</u> will we become kindly?

The subject of Hal's departure from the group is somberly aired. Each man has a special affinity with Hal and we fondly recount common memories of him. "Without Hal, do we seek additional members?" one man asks. Hal has left a gap. Quick responses:

"Not now."

"Hal cannot be replaced."

"Let's keep the group smaller."

"I like the group the size it is now."

Then we move on to another subject.

The evening ends when Joe explains he needs to get home to await a telephone call from his wife who is out of town at her cancer-beset daughter's bedside. Joe asks for prayers for Katie. His request is acknowledged, and we tell him we have been praying for Joe, his wife and Katie. Rather than let Joe slip away, each man rises and enfolds Joe in a corporate hug. There is power in that heartfelt group hug.

As men straggle off to respective vehicles for the trip home, conversations and fellowship accompany them outside. Lunches are set up for the following week. Family members are asked about and good wishes are sent their way. On clear, starry nights, Jim identifies stars and constellations as we direct our gazes heavenward. Final hugs are given. Good, warm feelings abound as we depart for home to share the sparks of camaraderie.

Each meeting is meaningful in some particular way for each of us. Bob's friendship and encouragement combined with the offer of a ride home convinced Hal to join. Hal had never experienced anything like the Barn Men. As we came to know him, he achieved a spot in everyone's heart. Who wouldn't admire an old fellow who walked the entire length of the Appalachian Trail one year; survived a tedious abdominal operation another, and the following year joined a footrace up Mt. Washington for the sole purpose of setting another record for eighty-five year olds?

Hal was the eldest member of the Barn Men and a no more compassionate resource of wisdom could be found. He was the elder-statesman for younger Barn Men. His long-time buddy, Jack, joined the Men a year or so ago. He brings unique outlooks as he shares inner workings of his interracial family, his life as a pastor and his perspectives on working at the Philadelphia Commission of Human Relations. Jack is assured he need not respond in his role as pastor at our meetings. Some months ago he shared a revealing incident with us. He explained that he had put considerable effort in preparing his African-American sons to deal with prejudice or discrimination inspired by false assumptions. He spoke of how false assumptions affect us all. He chuckled and told us of a recent experience. Jack and his nineteen year old granddaughter were walking on a center city street, their close relationship of love expressed by their entwined arms as they strolled on their way to hear the Philadelphia Orchestra. As they passed the steps leading to a business persons' club, a somewhat scruffy older African-American man who had been sitting there called out to Jack's granddaughter, "Young lady, you should be ashamed of yourself!"

Without response they continued on their way as they tried to absorb what had happened. After a few moments had gone by and they had time to think,

Jack realized the older observer's inaccurate assumption that Jack had picked up the young lady for something more than conversation. The older man's admonition was rooted in his concern for a young lady seemingly gone astray. And he was willing to step beyond his role as a stranger by speaking up. At that point Jack was upset with himself for not sorting things out before the moment for a response had passed. He recognizes that he should have stopped, introduced himself and his granddaughter and thanked the man for his concern and willingness to speak up.

When we heard Jack's story, we shared our attitudes about false assumptions. Most of us agreed our responses were not always what we would, after reflection, have liked them to have been and confessed that we had, at times, no doubt been guilty of false assumptions as well.

This was a wake up call for all of us.

Another night Jim, the philosopher, the fire-starter, painter and astronomer, used the analogy of his paints and pastels to speak of dark and light, painted and untouched canvas, good and evil and the juxtaposition of opposites as a means of gaining understanding. "If we experience only good, how could we ever recognize evil? How can we truly appreciate a sunrise with its manifold colors unless we have known a dark night?"

Health of self, immediate family members, distant and near friends are part of our conversations. Jim's idea of opposites gave rise to many tangents. Four of us have been diagnosed with cancer and the idea of opposites brought forth the concept, hard to grasp at first, that as we deal with this dreaded disease, there are consequent positives.

Jody led the way when his reply to, "How are you holding up?" after surgery and radiation was half over. "I just keep myself afloat on a day by day basis. I've learned to cross streams when I get to them and not spend a lot of time trying to figure out how to cross the damn things until I am close enough to figure out if there is a bridge, a ford or if I have to swim."

Jody's "just keeping myself afloat" became the refrain of another member, as he went through nine weeks of radiation.

What were the "star lights" the men found during their dark days battling cancer? Most often, the unexpected enlightenments concerned people. Witnessing the courage of fellow patients, making friends with strangers while sitting side by side in ill-fitting hospital gowns waiting for treatments, we pray there will be efficacious opportunities to see life as never before. The open, unabashed support of families and close friends makes cancer treatments "doable" and keep us afloat.

Receding libidos has been fodder for discussion at meetings. Ribald laughter would greet this topic in a different setting. Here the response was quiet reflection followed by frank conversation. It was a condition we all worried about and dealt with in various ways through abstinence or medically, with Viagra, but we drew comfort in sharing a seldom confronted male problem openly. No remedies are recommended, only genuine understanding.

A management task devolved to Bob of being a quiet steward of meeting process. He brings expertise in group dynamics. As a founder with Carter and Joe, Bob was entrusted with holding meetings to mutually agreed upon guidelines. Cutting through fluff, Bob reminds the group to be "present" and to speak from the "I" perspective. He gently guides speakers away from "you" and "we," to prefacing remarks with, "I think or I feel_____."

As he says of himself, "I have a keener appreciation for each man as I have come to know him over the course of years. I bring an intuitive disposition combined with enthusiasm and spiritual sensitivity to every meeting." Mote chides Bob when he enthusiastically proclaims cosmic, environmental events. He jokes that Bob is a "tree hugger extreme," but Mote often breaks evening silence with his own heartfelt cosmic observations emanating from Scripture. A contrarian in many ways, Mote provided varied views of familiar themes.

Close friends and companions for many years, Harry and Bill spring surprises. Harry enlivens conversation with insights learned from street people he befriends in the city. Years spent singing and playing the guitar come out poetically in questions and lyrical ideas.

Refreshing and vibrant, Harry brings an unusual dimension to the fellowship. The other member full of surprises is Bill, host of our meetings. We are fortunate that Bill generously shares the gardener's small, "office" at his home for our meetings. We can venture outside in pleasant seasons to smell spring coming, surrounded by fledglings who are as engaged in song as we are in conversation. On hot summer evenings we wish the sun down behind the tall trees; on evenings in the crisp early fall, scents bring anticipation of inviting fireside evenings. He provides our bucolic setting and is an amiable host.

We were surprised one evening last fall when our mild-mannered host was clearly annoyed and enumerated a number of irritations with us. We had scratched the meeting table. We expected him to provide the firewood. Someone unplugged the telephone. We didn't empty the garbage or sequester the recyclables. We had been oblivious and were surprised and sorry when he finally told us. We began to pull our load and he forgave us. But, the venting worked some magic for Bill. He became more outspoken. He even had to be reminded not to interrupt others. We had learned more about Bill; and Bill learned more about himself in the open exchange. Now he opens up and speaks out before he boils over.

His irritation helped all of us in being more attentive to the needs and expectations of others. Differences of opinion sometime lead to bent-out-of-shape feelings. A recent topic that resurfaces through the insistence of a couple of the men is to add more men to our group. Our numbers dwindle through death, moving away, advancing age, etc. Some members urge adding new members to achieve broader input for discussions and new people to bring in new energy and new breadth. Other Barn Men resist adding new members citing the comfort of known qualities of the present attendees. If nothing gets done to accommodate the differing opinions, a member can keep speaking up or his attendance fades off or he leaves the Barn Men.

To date we have accommodated these opposing feelings by tabling the rankling issue until all members are attendant. We find tabling a hot button topic for the next meeting helps. This gives everyone a chance to cool off and begin again. Taking disagreements home is a bad idea. Forming an alliance outside of meetings with one or two members has fractured similar groups and is strongly discouraged.

We are learning from each other, about each other—and in so doing we are learning to know ourselves better. The Barn men provide valuable support in gaining insights about issues that often remain buried below the surface. Unexplored notions percolate to the surface by virtue of the Barn Men's commitment to speak the truth, absent competition or accountability. As we engage with others in the charitable community of the Barn Men, we become wiser and better able to be the men we want to be.

The aim of banding together to accumulate wisdom through self-discovery in community for the purpose of propagating the wisdom and love among others is the greatest measure of success in a gathering of men. It is a measure that is visible in the lives of the men.

Nuggets For The Journey

During a meeting, sometimes after the go-round and before the silence, a member shares a reading. Our oral heritage offers many insights that quickly focus attention on themes for reflection. The following samples, some from Barn Men meetings, may give inspiration during a meeting or for individual reflection. More are available in *Gold Nuggets*, referenced at the end of this chapter.

"We do not choose the moment of our birth, who our parents will be, our particular culture, or the historical moment when we will be born...We are, as it were, thrown into existence with a challenge and a role that is beyond any personal choice. The nobility of our lives, however, depends upon the manner in which we come to understand and fulfill our assigned role."
Berry, Thomas. *The Great Work*, New York: Bell Tower, 2000.

Eternal Spirit,
Earth-maker, Pain-bearer, Life-giver,
Source of all that is and shall be,
Father and Mother of us all,
Loving God, in whom is heaven:
The hallowing of your name echo through the universe!

The way of your justice be followed by the peoples
of the world!
Your heavenly will be done by all created beings!
Your commonwealth of peace and freedom
sustain our hope and come on earth.
With the bread we need for today, feed us.
In the hurts we absorb from one another, forgive us.
In times of temptation and test, strengthen us.
From trials too severe to endure, spare us.
From the grip of all that is evil, free us.
For you rein in the glory of the power that is love,
now and for ever. Amen.

Alternative Lord's Prayer from Cotter, Jim. *Prayer at Night*. Sheffield, England: Cairns Publications, 1998. Reprinted with Permission.

"What you do with your suffering, when you are not in control, is at the heart of all healthy spirituality and all mature ministry."
"You Can Only Give What You Have Become" Richard Rohr, OFM, Radical Grace, Vol. 14, No. 3 July
2001, Center for Action and Contemplation, PO Box 12464, Albuquerque, NM 87195-2464

Start by doing what is necessary, then what is possible and suddenly you are doing "the impossible".
Saint Francis

To laugh is to risk appearing the fool,
To weep is to risk appearing sentimental,
To reach out for another is to risk involvement,
To expose our feelings is to risk exposing our true self,
To place our ideas and dreams before a crowd is to risk loss,
To love is to risk not being loved in return,
To live is to risk dying,
To hope is to risk despair,
To try at all is to risk failure,
But risk we must, because the greatest hazard in life is to risk nothing.
The man, the woman who risks nothing, does nothing, has nothing,
is nothing.
Anonymous

Do you think you are a mistake…just because you made one?
Anonymous

When I ask you to listen to me and you start giving advice, you have not done what I asked.
When I ask you to listen to me and you begin to tell me
why I shouldn't feel that way, you are trampling on my feelings.
When I ask you to listen to me and you feel you have to do something to solve my problem, you have failed me, strange as that may seem.
Listen! All I asked was that you listen, not talk or do—just hear me.

Advice is cheap; fifteen cents will get you both Dear Abby and Billy Graham
in the same newspaper.
And I can do for myself. I am not helpless. Maybe discouraged and faltering,
but not helpless.
When you do something for me that I can and need to do for myself, you
contribute to my fear and inadequacy.

But, when you accept as a simple fact that I do feel what I feel, no matter how
irrational, then I can quit trying to convince you and can get about this business
of understanding what's behind this irrational feeling.
And when that's clear, the answers are obvious and I don't need advice.
Irrational feelings make sense when we understand what's behind them.
Perhaps that's why prayer works, sometimes, for some people—because God
is mute, and he/she doesn't give advice or try to fix things. "They" just
listen and let you work it out for yourself.
So listen and just hear me. And, if you want to talk, wait a minute for your turn,
and I'll listen to you.
Author Unknown

The pessimist looks at opportunities and see difficulties.
The optimist looks at difficulties and sees opportunities.
Author Unknown

We read in the papers, we hear on the air
Of killing and stealing, of crime everywhere.
We sigh and we say as we notice the trend,
"This young generation, when will it end?"
But can we be sure that it's their fault alone,
That maybe most of it isn't really our own?
Too much money to spend, too much idle time,
Too many movies of passion and crime,
Too many books not fit to be read,
Too much of evil in what they hear said,
Too many children encouraged to roam,
By too many parents who won't stay home.
Kids don't make the movies, they don't write the books
that paint a gay picture of gangsters and crooks.

They don't make the liquor, they don't run the bars, they
don't pass the laws nor make high-speed cars.
They don't make the drugs that addle the brain.
It's all done by older folks greedy for gain.
Thus, in so many cases it must be confessed,
The label, delinquent, fits older folks best.
Author Unknown

In a sense, we place the same burdens on our organizational life as we place o the
rest of our existence. We feel there is something wrong at the center of it all, and
we have to put it right. We are forever looking for a cure for our ills. We do this
by placing ourselves in the position of *manager*, of thus *managing* change. Unless
it is managed, something is wrong. But our real unconscious and underlying wish
is to find a cure for the impermanence of life, and for that there is no remedy.
Most of the difficulties we confront at work are no different from those human
beings have been dealing with for millennia. Life is full of loneliness, failure, grief
and loss to an extent that terrifies us, and we will do anything to will ourselves
another existence.
Whyte, David. *The Heart Arroused.* New York: Currency Doubleday, 1994.
Pp280–281

We have forgotten the poise that comes from living in storied relation and reci-
procity with the myriad things, the myriad *beings*, that perceptually surround us.
Abram, David. *The Spell of the Sensuous.* New York: Vintage Books, 1996, p.
270.

It's time we looked instead at the unquestioned answers, and the biggest, most
unquestioned answer of our culture is our relationship with money. It is there
that we keep alive—at a high cost—the flame and mythology of scarcity.
Twist, Lynne. *The Soul of Money.* New York: W. W. Norton & Company, Inc,
2003, p. 66.

Around the corner I have a friend,
In this great city that has no end,
Yet the days go by and weeks rush on,
And before I know it, a year is gone.
And I never see my old friends face,
For life is a swift and terrible race,

He knows I like him just as well,
As in the days when I rang his bell.
And he rang mine but we were younger then,
And now we are busy, tired men.
Tired of playing a foolish game,
Tired of trying to make a name.

"Tomorrow" I say! "I will call on Jim
Just to show that I'm thinking of him."
But tomorrow comes and tomorrow goes,
And distance between us grows and grows.
Around the corner, yet miles away,
"Here's a telegram sir," "Jim died today."
And that's what we get and deserve in the end.
Around the corner, a vanished friend.
Remember to always say what you mean. If you love someone, tell them.
Don't be afraid to express yourself.
Reach out and tell someone what they mean to you. Because when you decide
that it is the right time it might be too late.
Seize the day.
Never have regrets.
And most important, stay close to your friends and family, for they have helped
make you the person that you are today.

Anonymous

Recommended Reading

Berry, Thomas. *The Great Work*. New York: Bell Tower, 1999

Berry, Thomas and Swimme, Brian. *The Universe Story*. New York: Harper Collins, 1992

Robert Bly, James Hillman, and Michael Meade

The Rag and Bone Shop of the Heart; Poems for Men. New York: Harper Collins, 1992

Brown, Thomas. *Vision*. East Rutherford, NJ: Berkley Publishing, 1991

Campbell, Joseph with Moyers, Bill. *The Power of Myth*. New York: Doubleday, 1988

Coelho, Mary Conrow. *Awakening Universe, Emerging Personhood, The Power of Contemplation in an Evolving Universe*. Lima, Ohio: Wyndham Hall Press, 2002

Frankl, Victor E. *Man's Search for Meaning*. Old Tappan, NJ: Touchstone Books, 1984

Kabat-Zinn, Jon. *Wherever You Go There You Are—Mindfulness Meditation in Everyday Life*. New York: Hyperion, 1994

Kelly, Thomas R. *A Testament of Devotion*. San Francisco, CA: Harper San Francisco, 1941

Macdonald, Copthorne. *Matters of Consequence*. Charlottetown, Prince Edward Island, Canada: Big Ideas Press, 2004

Moore, Robert and Gillette, Douglas. *King Warrior Magician Lover: Rediscovering the Archetypes of Mature Masculine*. SanFrancisco, CA: Harper Collins, 1990

Oliver, Mary. *New and Selected Poems*. Boston: Beacon Press, 1992

Orion, a bimonthly publication of the Orion Society and the Myrin Institute, 187 Main St., Great Barrington, MA. Website: www.oriononline.org.

Ray, Paul H. Ph.D. and Anderson, Sherry Ruth Ph.D. *The Cultural Creative: How 50 Million People Are Changing the World*. New York: Three Rivers Press, 2000

Real, Terrence. *How Can I Get Through to You?* New York: Scribner, 2002

Rezendes, Paul. *The Wild Within*. New York: Berkley Books, 1998

Resurgence, a bimonthly publication from Cornwall, UK. Website: www. resurgence.org.

Rohr, Richard and Martos, Joseph. *The Wild Man's Journey: Reflections on Male Spirituality*.

Cincinnati, Ohio: St. Anthony Messenger Press, 1992

Tannen, Deborah. *That Is Not What I Meant! How Conversational Style Makes or Breaks Your Relations with Others*. Westminster, MD: Valentine Books, 1991

The Earth Charter. Website: www.earthcharter.org

Timeline, a bimonthly publication of the Foundation for Global Community, 222 High St., Palo Alto, CA. Website: www.Globalcommunity.org

Williams, Terry Tempest. *The Open Space of Democracy*. Great Barrington, MA: The Orion Society, 2004

Origin of the Twisting Flame Symbol

During a gathering Lew Mills asked me, "How would you paint the men's group?".
At first I thought he meant portraits.
"Symbolically, "he said.
I looked at the candle on the table with the group seated around it and said, "A flame in a circle".

After Lew passed on, I was asked to design a bronze plaque to be mounted on a memorial bench at St. David's Churchyard. I began by considering many encircled flame designs and selected one which shows a wisp of flame that twists as it rises, suggesting the turning over and the flicker of ideas. The circumference line breaks into itself and spires upward twisting to reveal the inner light we all possess—a glimpse of truth that comes from contemplating the ever-changing infinite moment.

Jim Simmons

About the Authors

The three authors do share many similar elements in their backgrounds. All are university graduates. All have traveled widely. All were teachers in one form or another. **Lew Mills** was an active and outreaching pastor. Both **Derek Stedman** and **Bob Wallis** were teachers. Derek Stedman has taught from elementary school grades through graduate level teaching at Widener University. Bob Wallis worked in the Peace Corps after he graduated from college. Each author has especially wide associations with other people from many walks of life. Each has enjoyed first-hand experiences working collaboratively with varied people in varying circumstances. This delight and excitement of being with and talking with others created the incentives for writing this book together to aid and abet meaningful conversations, particularly among men and their families.

A love of the outdoors is a common thread among the authors. Hiking, camping, sailing, gardening and purposefully interacting with diverse acquaintances are among the shared enjoyments. Each author has belonged to varieties of groups of people through formal work groups serving a set purpose to committee efforts through community or religious affiliations. Each author married, divorced and re-married. Thus each has the special gift of sharing his life and work with his own children and those of his spouse. Each is a grandfather; that, too, is special as each generation gets to know a wider and more diverse family group. All of these similarities give rise to the core question: what must we authors share with other men and their families in order for each person in a family of different generations to understand each other better?

What makes *A Gathering of Men* unique is that there is no other known book quite like it. The book takes the reader through the early stages eleven years ago to the Barn Men's present status. We are now seven men, including two founders, who are all dedicated to thoughtfully replenishing membership with the addition of a few newcomers who are diverse in backgrounds yet who are "committed to searching for wisdom and shared truths about life". During part of 2005 and 2006 one of the founders of the Barn Men was being taken from his family, multitudes of friends and the Barn Men by cancer. It just did not seem appropriate for the other members of the Barn Men to spread their energies seeking new members while one so dear to each of us needed the efforts of the Barn Men to be focused on him and his family.

978-0-595-40865-8
0-595-40865-6